CHRISTIANS WHO CHANGED THE WORLD

CHRISTIANS WHO CHANGED THE WORLD

Clare Richards

Illustrated by Donald Melvin

Kevin Mayhew

First published in 2001 by
KEVIN MAYHEW LTD
Buxhall, Stowmarket, Suffolk IP14 3BW
E-mail: info@kevinmayhewltd.com

9 8 7 6 5 4 3 2 1 0

ISBN 1 84003 857 8
Catalogue No 1500483

Cover design by Angela Selfe
Edited and typeset by Elisabeth Bates
Printed in Great Britain

CONTENTS

Foreword 7
Introduction 9

Jesus of Nazareth 11

Section 1: Prayer

St Benedict 13
Julian of Norwich 17
St Teresa of Avila 19
St Thérèse of Lisieux 19
Brother Roger of Taizé 23
Summary on prayer 26

Section 2: Poverty

William Booth 27
St Francis of Assisi 31
Clare Fey 33
Charles de Foucauld 37
Little Sister Magdeleine 37
Summary on poverty 40

Section 3: Teaching

St Matthew 41
St Luke 45
St Thomas Aquinas 47
St Dominic 47
John Wesley 51
Charles Wesley 51
Summary on teaching 55

Section 4: Healing

St Vincent de Paul 57
St Louise de Marillac 58
Albert Schweitzer 61
Father Damien 62
Mother Teresa 65
Diana, Princess of Wales 65
Dame Cicely Saunders 68
Dr Sheila Cassidy 68
Summary on healing 72

Section 5: Equality

William Wilberforce 73
Lord Shaftesbury 74
Trevor Huddleston 77
Martin Luther King 81
Sojourner Truth 81
Harriet Tubman 82
Sean Devereux 85
Stephanie Pinnington 85
Summary on equality 88

Section 6: Justice

Julian Filochowski 89
Sister Ita Ford 93
Jaime Jaramilo 95
Camilo Torres 96
Chico Mendes 99
Rigoberta Menchu 99
Summary on justice 103

Section 7: Peace

Dietrich Bonhoeffer 105
Franz Jaegerstaetter 107
David Trimble and John Hume 111
Mairead Corrigan and Betty Williams 112
Mary McAleese 115
Summary on peace 117

Section 8: Take Up Your Cross

St Stephen 119
St Thomas More 120
Thomas Cranmer 120
St Mark 123
St Maximilian Kolbe 125
Archbishop Oscar Romero 129
Summary on 'take up your cross' 131

Section 9: Forgiveness

Elizabeth Fry 133
Helen Prejean 135
Gordon Wilson 139
Elias Chacour 139
Archbishop Desmond Tutu 143
Summary on forgiveness 145

Section 10: Leaders

St Peter 147
Pope John XXIII 149
St Paul 153
Martin Luther 155
Summary on leaders 158

Mary, Mother of Jesus 159

Conclusion 163

Index 165
Acknowledgements 167

FOREWORD

We are all aware how events can change the world. As I write this foreword we are still in shock over the tragic events of 11 September 2001 when the World Trade Center in New York was reduced to dust. Everyone agrees that the world will never be the same again.

The world seems to move from one horror to another. It is now focused in Afghanistan, where millions of lives are threatened by hunger, frozen winter conditions and war. But there is always the promise of hope and a 'resurrection' from the suffering and death. That hope is realised when individuals stand out from the crowd by their courage, vision and persistence, often against all odds. This book is about Christian heroes who have changed the world in this way.

The Gospels give us an insight into the man, Jesus, whom his followers were later to describe as the true Son of God, the Christ. His example and teaching were radical and threatened the comfortable authorities and men of religious power. They didn't like to be challenged. Who does?

It seems to me, therefore, that people who really live the Gospel have to disturb others. They are revolutionaries. Christ asked his followers to make a selfish world more generous – a task which is not very popular. But individuals have always found ways to shake others out of apapthy; even out of selfish hatred of others. These are the Christian heroes that I am writing about.

These Christians who really live the Gospel walk on a knife-edge because they claim to be both in the world and yet not of it. My husband, Bert, has been writing about this recently. He writes: *'We seldom get the balance right. We are often so identified with the world that we cannot speak to it, and at other times so remote from it that again we are unable to speak to it. To practise holy worldliness means to walk on a constant knife-edge. We fall off it when we are either too worldly or too other-worldly. In neither case are we practising holiness.'*

Some Christians, over the ages, have managed to get the balance just right. In doing so their lives have actually changed the world. They have, in extraordinary ways, brought peace where there was anguish, joy where there was misery, 'richness' where there was poverty and life where there was death.

I'd like to dedicate this book to those young people of today who have the courage to speak out against injustice and inequality. There is much to challenge in our world. Maybe some of you who read this book will be encouraged to speak up and make a difference.

Clare Richards

INTRODUCTION

In the 1920s a young Russian boy, living in Paris, was struggling to understand the purpose and meaning of life. He hated any suggestion that a God existed and he was 'very aggressively anti-church'. When the leader of his youth club invited a priest to talk to the group, Anthony was indignant and at first refused to attend. He went in the end only because all his friends had decided to go. He was infuriated by the priest's description of Christianity so he went home and asked his mother for a copy of the New Testament. He wanted to prove that the whole Jesus story was utter nonsense.

Anthony chose to read Mark's Gospel because it was the shortest. Then something dramatic happened. As he read, chapter by chapter the person of Jesus became real to him. He wrote later: *'I suddenly became aware that on the other side of the desk there was a presence. And the certainty was so strong that it was Christ standing there, that it has never left me.'* The boy was so influenced by the Gospel that he later became a monk, then a priest and today is known as Archbishop Anthony Bloom, leader of the Russian Orthodox Church in England.

Archbishop Anthony points out that an earlier experience as an 11-year-old had prepared him for his 'conversion'. On a boys' summer camp he had met a priest whom he found 'extremely puzzling'. He seemed to have an unconditional ability to love everyone, whether they were good or bad. Young Anthony hadn't met this kind of generosity before. Later, Anthony could see the connection between this priest and the Gospel. He said: *'Only years later, when I had already discovered the Gospel, did it occur to me that he loved with a love that was beyond him. He shared out divine love to us, or if you prefer, his human love was of such depth and had such scope and scale that he could include all of us, either through joy or pain, but still within one love.'*

This is a good explanation of Christian living. All Christians believe in the resurrection of Jesus, the Son of God. One aspect of resurrection is the continual presence of Christ in the world, in the lives of ordinary people. Sometimes ordinary people seem to act with a love, compassion or forgiveness that seems beyond the humanly possible. In this book I have chosen a cross section of these people who bring Christianity to life. They are people who have found the life and teaching of Jesus an inspiration for their own lives. Of course they believe that Jesus is more than just an inspiring figure to imitate. They accept him into their lives as the Son of God, and they celebrate his life and follow his teaching by being members of the Church with all its traditions, customs and beliefs. Other books look at these aspects of Christianity. I want, quite simply, to show how Jesus lives on in the lives of outstanding Christians. The lives of many Christians down the ages shine with holiness. Being holy is being Christ-like. That is why we can see their lives reflected in the pages of the Gospels, where the early Church recorded and reflected on the life of Jesus Christ, the Son of God. Some Christian denominations (Roman Catholic and Orthodox) officially recognise some of these outstanding Christians by calling them Saints. Although Paul, the earliest Christian writer, addressed all followers of Jesus as saints.

One day, about 60 years ago, a young South African boy called Desmond was walking with his mother through a black township. He was astonished when a white priest took his hat off and greeted them warmly. White people did not talk to his people. The English priest was Trevor Huddleston. Later, when the boy spent a long time in hospital with tuberculosis, Father Trevor visited him and his family. It was this kindness that influenced Desmond for the rest of his life. He thought deeply about the Christian faith that inspired the priest and he followed in his footsteps. Both were to become bishops in the Anglican Church. Archbishop Desmond Tutu eventually became an outstanding international figure for peace and justice.

Archbishop Bloom and Archbishop Desmond Tutu both discovered a need to belong to the Christian community by meeting outstanding Christians who, in turn, directed them to the Gospels to find God in the person of Jesus Christ.

JESUS OF NAZARETH

Introduction

The year 2000 celebrated the second millennium (millennium means one thousand years). It is 2000 years, roughly, since the birth of Jesus of Nazareth, known as Jesus the Christ. His followers became known as Christians. The Millennium is primarily a Christian celebration.

Jesus was born in a humble family and lived in a small town called Nazareth, in Palestine. Today this land is known as Israel. He was a Jewish boy who became a local carpenter and then a preacher. His teaching was found unacceptable by the authorities and so he was condemned to death. He died nailed to a cross, between two criminals.

Accounts of Jesus' life and teaching are recorded in the four **Gospels.** The word means '**Good News**'. How can death by crucifixion be considered 'good news'? Christians throughout the 2000 years have believed that Jesus' death was only the beginning of his story. Jesus was raised from the dead and continues to live in the believing community - the Church - through the Holy Spirit. This is the 'Good News'.

How does Jesus live on in the Church? One way is through ordinary people. The Church is made up of people. Individual followers of Jesus, his **disciples**, try to imitate his life and base their ideals on his teaching. Jesus lives on when their lives reflect his. In this book we are going to look at some of these Christian disciples of Jesus.

Disciples of Jesus

When Jesus preached in the towns and countryside of Palestine 2000 years ago he attracted many followers, both men and women. They listened to his teaching about the **Kingdom of God** and then tried to follow this way of living. They became his disciples. From this group Jesus chose twelve men as special friends. He sent them out to teach the Good News about God's Kingdom. We call them the **Apostles**, a Greek word which means 'sent on a mission'. When Jesus died these men became the first leaders of the Christian community - the early Church.

The Church

Christians today no longer form one single group of believers in Jesus Christ. There are many different groups, or **denominations**, of Christians. Roman Catholics make up the largest group and many people described in this book are from this Christian Church. Others are from the Anglican Church, Eastern Orthodox Churches, the Lutheran Church, the Baptist Church, the Methodist Church, the Evangelical Movement, the Salvation Army and the Society of Friends (Quakers). Christian denominations are divided by their different beliefs, but the Gospel itself continues to unite all Christians in a common faith and vision.

Who was Jesus?

'Who do the crowds say I am?' he asked them.
'Some say that you are John the Baptist;
others say that you are Elijah . . .'
'What about you? Who do you say I am?'
Peter answered, 'You are God's Messiah'.
Luke 9:18-20

When Jesus was alive people were always asking who he claimed to be. People still ask that question today. The Gospel writers believed he was quite unique. They gave to Jesus a number of titles.

MESSIAH This is the Hebrew word for **anointed one**. The Greek word for Messiah is **CHRIST**.

Jesus the Messiah (Hebrew)
Jesus the Christ (Greek)
Jesus the Anointed One (English)

The Old Testament gave this title to all the Israelite kings. A *messiah* was someone chosen and anointed for a special leadership task. When there were no more Israelite kings, the people looked forward to a future king who would bring them peace.

SON OF DAVID This is a rare title. The Jews expected the future messiah to be a descendant of their favourite king, King David. He had been their greatest leader and had made Jerusalem their capital city. He came from Bethlehem, the eventual birthplace of Jesus.

SON OF GOD This title was also given to the kings. They claimed they had been chosen by God to rule in his place. Jesus is often given this title in the Gospel.

SON OF MAN This title has supernatural overtones. It was used in the Book of Daniel as a symbol of a better future. Later writers described the Son of Man as a heavenly figure coming in clouds down to earth. Jesus often used this title about himself.

JESUS THE LORD This can simply mean 'Sir', but it is also used in the Old Testament instead of 'Yahweh', the name given to God himself.

It would seem that the first Christians were not altogether clear who Jesus was. But by the end of the first century they had given him all these titles. They knew he was unique. Christians today still discuss what the titles mean.

Jesus and the Kingdom of God

Jesus taught his disciples through stories, known as **parables**. Many of them started with the words, *'The Kingdom of God is like . . .'* The Gospel writers recorded many of the stories, and so we have several pictures of how Jesus saw God's Kingdom. Jesus made it very clear that the Kingdom of God was not just a hope for the future – it had already arrived on earth.

What is the Kingdom of God like?
The Kingdom of God means God's Rule, or God's Way. And God's Way is one of LOVE, FORGIVE-NESS, COMPASSION.

Where is God's Kingdom?
It is not an earthly kingdom with leaders, boundaries and a police force. It is not the same as heaven – in the future. But it is something existing now, and to be completed in the future.

Who is in God's Kingdom?
The Kingdom is for everybody. All are welcome. But it is most especially open to the poor, outcasts, sinners and the dispossessed.

Summary

Jesus lived a life full of love, forgiveness and compassion. He showed this by example and by the way he taught, free of prejudice and selfishness. **In him the Kingdom of God had already been established on earth.** Whenever people live in the same way as Jesus, following his example and teaching, **they are already in the Kingdom**. But it is not easy. It is like entering through a very narrow door (see Luke 13:22-30).

Disciples of Jesus try to follow his example and listen to his words. In the following pages we will see how, through the ages, Christian disciples have built their lives around Gospel texts which inspired them.

1. *Jesus took Peter, John and James with him and went up a hill to pray.* Luke 9:28
2. *Go and sell all you have . . . give to the poor . . . then come and follow me.* Mark 10:21
3. *Go, then, to all peoples everywhere and make them my disciples.* Matthew 28:19
4. *Jesus healed many who were sick with all kind of diseases.* Mark 1:34
5. *Do for others just what you want them to do for you.* Luke 6:31
6. *Do not judge others, and God will not judge you.* Luke 6:37
7. *Love your enemies and pray for those who persecute you.* Matthew 5:44
8. *Whoever does not carry his own cross . . . cannot be my disciple.* Luke 14:27
9. *Forgive them, Father! They don't know what they are doing.* Luke 23:34
10. *If one of you wants to be first, he must be the slave of all.* Mark 10:44

SECTION 1: PRAYER

Jesus took Peter, John and James with him and went up a hill to pray

Luke 9:28

Introduction

In this section we look at four Christians who made prayer the centre of their lives. Each one recognised that Jesus was their model and each one found a way to 'get in touch with themselves at a deeper level than usual'.

The simplest description of prayer is 'talking to God' and 'listening to God'. Christians believe that God can be discovered and reached when people learn how to recognise the quietness of their deepest selves. That is why prayer is not just repeating words. An early saint, John Chrysostom, said: *'When you discover the door of your heart you discover the gate of heaven.'*

Damian Lundy, a twentieth-century Christian, put it this way: *'Prayer is getting in touch with God. This means getting in touch with ourselves at a rather deeper level than usual.'* He had in mind the words of St Paul: *'Do you not know that your body is a temple of the Holy Spirit, who is in you, whom you have received from God?'* 1 Corinthains 6:19

A Russian archbishop, Anthony Bloom, explains this in these words: *'Prayer is born of the discovery that the world has depths; that we are not only surrounded by visible things but that we are also immersed in and penetrated by invisible things. And this invisible world is both the presence of God, the supreme, sublime reality, and our own deepest truth.'*

ST BENEDICT

Feast: 11 July

The monastic rule of St Benedict is a sixth-century document which has never gathered dust. It is relevant in every age because its followers are led to Christ.

Benet Tvedten OSB

Benedict was born in Nursia, Italy. We do not know very much about his youth except that he left home at 14, and went to study in Rome. He hated the wild, immoral life of the Roman people of that time, so when he was about 18 he fled from the city into the desert. He joined some hermits in Subiaco. After a few years, known for his holiness and wisdom, he was invited by local monks to join their community. Over a number of years he founded twelve small monasteries, including one on Monte Cassino. From there he wrote his '**Rule**' for the monastic life of prayer, study and work.

Benedict was a peaceful, determined and respected man. Although he asked for absolute obedience to the Rule, he was a gentle father to the monks. He respected them as individuals and only asked what was possible, and practical. He wrote:

The saying is that monks ought not to drink wine. But since today no monk believes this, let us at least drink in moderation. Rule 515

When he was dying Benedict was taken to the chapel to receive communion for the last time. He died at the altar and was buried in the same grave as his twin sister, Scholastica, *'so death did not separate the bodies of these two, whose minds had ever been united in the Lord'*. She had lived a similar life of prayer to her brother, and died four years before him.

The Rule of St Benedict

The Rule that Benedict wrote became the model for all western monks and nuns for centuries. In fact, this monastic system of Benedict preserved religion, promoted the arts, science and even agriculture in Europe throughout a time (known as the Dark Ages) when the world was in some disarray.

Monks live a community life which is centred around their daily celebration of the Eucharist. They meet at other times in the day to pray as a community, and they spend some hours in private prayer and study, based on the Scriptures. Benedict encouraged his monks to be self-sufficient, so all of them take part in physical work: teaching, gardening, cooking, writing, wine-making or welcoming guests to the monastery.

Benedictines today

The Benedictine Order has a strong presence in the Roman Catholic and Anglican Churches today. Great abbeys, like Downside Abbey and the nuns of Stanbrook Abbey, share their tradition of monastic prayer with a wider world. Their prayer, sung in Gregorian chant and choral music, is now sold on disc. Dom Dunstan O'Keeffe of Downside wrote:

> *In offering praise to God through music, the monastic community both performs its most important work and expresses its hidden life of prayer. The rhythm of the chant is the rhythm of a life that is ordered to the things of God.*
>
> Introduction to *Gregorian Moods*, Virgin Records, 1997

Downside Abbey and Stanbrook Abbey are Roman Catholic foundations. There are five Anglican Benedictine monastaries in England and there are enclosed Anglican Benedictine nuns at West Malling in Kent.

Although many monks and nuns are **contemplative**, and live an enclosed life within the monastery, some are involved in education. The Benedictines have a long tradition of teaching in schools attached to the monasteries. Ampleforth College in Yorkshire is a great example of a flourishing monastic boarding school for boys. The school is rich in the Benedictine tradition.

Benedict was born over 1500 years ago yet the style of monastic life he introduced remains popular even today. Why is this? Perhaps it is because every person needs some quietness in their life. In Italy today some travel magazines are even offering monastic 'vacations'. Over a dozen Benedictine Abbeys are welcoming holiday-makers, inviting them to take advantage of the peace and quiet they have to offer.

What the Scriptures say:

> *At once the Spirit made him go into the desert where he stayed forty days, being tempted by Satan. Wild animals were there also, but angels came and helped him.* Mark 1:12-13

> *Very early, long before daylight, Jesus got up and left the house. He went out of the town to a lonely place, where he prayed.* Mark 1:35

What the Churches say:

> *Prayer is the key to open the day, and the bolt to shut-in the night.* John Hackett in *Christian Consolations*, AD 1671

Summary

480 born in Nursia

494 sent to study in Rome

498 fled Rome to Subiaco and lived as a hermit

501 began building monasteries

525 established Monte Cassino and wrote his Rule

547 Died

Quick questions

1. What is prayer?
2. Anthony Bloom says *'prayer is born of a discovery…'* What is the discovery?
3. What is monastic life?
4. In what way are Benedictine monks following Jesus' life?

ROME
AUSCULTA
RULE
MONTE CASSINO
BENEDICT
B. 480 D. 547

NORWICH
IPSWICH
LONDON
JULIAN OF NORWICH • B• 1342 • D• AFTER • 1416 •

JULIAN OF NORWICH

Feast: 8 May (Anglican calendar)

It is God's will that we should know him, and his pleasure that we should rest in him. Nothing less will satisfy us.
Julian, in Revelations, chapter 5

To know the goodness of God is the highest prayer of all.
Julian, in Revelations, chapter 6

In the fourteenth century the Benedictine nuns had a monastery at Carrow in Norwich (on a site near Norwich City Football Club at Carrow Road). It was usual for some men and women to live outside the communities as recluses, or **anchoresses**. It is thought that Julian of Norwich was one of these, living a solitary life in a special cell attached to the church of St Julian (which accounts for her name).

Little detail is known about her, but she was the first woman to write a book in English. It is possible to guess something of what she was like from her writings. She had more formal learning than most fourteenth-century women. Her deep understanding of what it means to be a mother (she describes God as mother) suggests she came from a happy home and may even have been a young wife who lost her husband and children when the plague devastated Norwich in 1361 and 1369.

When Julian was about 30 years old she was very ill and close to death. At this time she had a number of revelations of the love of God and visions of Christ on the cross. It may have been these prayerful insights into the mystery of God that made her decide to become an anchoress. She recovered and lived alongside the church for many years. There she devoted her life to prayer and meditation on the Scriptures, and wrote about her revelations. During these years Mother Julian (she was also called Dame and Lady) is known to have received many visitors who sought guidance and encouragement in their spiritual lives.

Julian reached a high degree of perfection in prayer and holiness. She is regarded as a **mystic**. In other words, she discovered the *'invisible world as both the presence of God, the supreme, sublime reality, and her own deepest truth'* (from Anthony Bloom).

Living the solitary life as a recluse is an unusual response to the Christian Gospel. But there have always been men and women who choose this way of life. Today there is another recluse living in Norfolk, not too far from Norwich. She is Sister Wendy, the nun who writes about art and who has occasionally left her isolated caravan to appear on television.

What the Scriptures say:

When you pray, go to your room, close the door, and pray to your Father, who is unseen. Matthew 6:6

After sending the crowds away he went up into the hills by himself to pray. Matthew 14:23

But he would go away to lonely places, where he prayed. Luke 5:16

What the Churches and Christians say:

Prayer is recognising, to use some ancient words, that the Most High has made not one world but two. In our secular world we have never been so technically competent, but the longing for the other world of faith, the desire to grasp truth through the imagination, has never been stronger.
Alan Webster, former Dean of St Paul's

Different forms of prayer

The Christian tradition describes three major expressions or forms of prayer:

1. **Vocal Prayer**
   Human beings are body and soul (spirit) which means that inner experience needs to be expressed outwardly by voice and gesture. Jesus taught his disciples vocal prayer, the **Lord's Prayer**.
2. **Meditation**
   This is reflection, using the mind to search for understanding, and using the emotions to respond in feeling and desire for God. Reading and thinking about the Scriptures can be at the heart of this form of prayer.
3. **Contemplation**
   Contemplation was described perfectly many years ago by a humble peasant. Asked what he did, sitting at the back of the church, he replied: *'I look at him and he looks at me'.* Contemplation can lead to mystical experience.

The medieval mystics

Julian is one of a number of medieval mystics of the fourteenth and fifteenth centuries. Mysticism is the spiritual search (in any religion) for a direct experience of God. Mystics concentrate on prayer, meditation, contemplation and fasting. This appears to be the way that individuals develop the attitude and faith necessary for this direct encounter with God.

Christian mystics, like Julian, focus on the suffering of Jesus in their prayer. Another Christian mystic of the fourteenth century was Margery Kempe of Lynn who actually visited Julian for advice. Other well-known mystics include St Francis of Assisi (see page 31) and St Teresa of Avila (see page 19).

Summary

1342 Born in Norwich

1349 The Black Death (plague)

1361 Another outbreak of plague

1369 Plague again in Norwich

1373 Julian is very ill and has her Revelations

1381 Peasants' Revolt, especially in East Anglia

1416 Julian is mentioned in a will (so still alive). It is not known when she died

Quick questions

1. What does the writing of Julian tell us about her?
2. Describe three different expressions of prayer. Write two sentences on each.
3. What is mysticism?
4. How does a recluse (anchoress) follow the example of Jesus?

ST TERESA OF AVILA

Feast: 15 October

Let nothing disturb you,
nothing alarm you;
while all things fade away
God is unchanging.

Mount Carmel is in Israel and is associated with the prophet Elijah. A small group of European hermits settled there. In the thirteenth century an English hermit, Simon Stock, devised a rule for these 'Carmelite' monks and nuns and spread their way of life throughout Europe.

Three centuries later a lively, well-educated young Spanish woman entered a Carmelite monastery in Avila. It was an easy-going, comfortable community but the young nun made for herself a serious life of prayer and contemplation. She became a mystic and visionary, not unlike Julian of Norwich. But she was practical, spontaneous and energetic. Against opposition she founded a new monastery in 1562. She returned it to the original strict rule of Carmel. She then founded another eighteen monasteries and wrote books about her life and on prayer. She was a forceful, charming woman, *a pioneering feminist,* who deeply influenced the Church and laid foundations for the study of human psychology. She had faults, but also an overwhelming love of God.

St Thérèse of Lisieux

Three hundred years later a young French girl, Thérèse, walked naturally in the footsteps of the great Spanish Carmelite. In 1888 the 15-year-old Thérèse entered a Carmelite monastery in Lisieux, Northern France. She died of TB only nine years later, after what seemed an uneventful, ordinary and very hidden life. She only became known outside her convent because she was asked to write an account of her life. The autobiography became a published best-seller under the title *The Story of a Soul.* Its great appeal was its assurance that the most ordinary person could reach holiness. Thérèse's whole life was motivated by the desire to love God through doing daily humdrum tasks as well as she could. In this way she made every moment a kind of prayer.

Only twenty-eight years after her death the Roman Catholic Church pronounced her a saint.

What the Scriptures say:

My commandment is this. Love one another, just as I love you. John 15:12

The Spirit also comes to help us, weak as we are. For we do not know how we ought to pray; the Spirit himself pleads with God for us in groans that words cannot express. Romans 8:26

The Prayer of the Church

All monks and nuns meet at regular times to pray the **Prayer of the Church**. This pattern of prayer is sometimes called *The Divine Office.* Its purpose is to set aside certain times of the day for prayer in the community. Some monks and nuns meet five times a day to pray together.

LAUDS:	Morning prayer
LITTLE HOURS:	Midday prayer (used to be in three parts, Terce, Sext and None)
VESPERS:	Evening prayer
COMPLINE:	Night prayer
MATINS:	Readings at a suitable community time

The heart of the prayers is expressed in psalms, canticles, Scripture readings, responses and prayers of intercession. These change in the course of the liturgical year. This *Divine Office* is intended to be public prayer for the whole Church. Priests in parishes take part in it using a book called the *Breviary.* Some churches invite their parishioners to join in Morning and Evening Prayer. It is often sung in Anglican cathedrals.

Active Sisters

The Benedictine and Carmelite way of life is known as 'contemplative'. The monks and nuns live in monasteries, devoting their lives to work, study and prayer. There are many thousands of nuns today who live more active lives, teaching, nursing the sick or caring for people on the margins of society.

These active Sisters, like Mother Teresa (see page 65) and Clare Fey (see page 33) belong to 'religious congregations' which are based on the older monastic orders. All nuns, Anglican, Roman Catholic and Orthodox, pray the Divine Office. They find in prayer the strength to work for others.

A psalm of praise: Psalm 150

Praise God in his Temple!
Praise his strength in heaven!
Praise him for the mighty things he has done.
Praise his supreme greatness.

Praise him with trumpets.
Praise him with harps and lyres.
Praise him with drums and dancing.
Praise him with harps and flutes.

Praise him with cymbals.
Praise him with loud cymbals.
Praise the Lord, all living creatures!

Praise the Lord!

Summary

Thirteenth century: St Simon Stock brought the Carmelite Order into Europe

1515 Teresa of Avila was born

1535 She entered Carmel

1562 She reformed the Order

1582 She died

1873 Thérèse of Lisieux born

1888 She entered Carmel

1897 She died

1925 She was proclaimed Saint

Quick questions

1. Outline the history of the Carmelite Order.
2. Why do you think Teresa of Avila has been called a *pioneering feminist*?
3. Describe the *Divine Office*.

THERESE OF LISIEUX B 1873 D 1897
SALAMANCA
PEÑARANDA
AVILA
TERESA OF AVILA B 1515 D 1582

ZURICH
BERN
CHALON
E1
TOURNUS
TAIZÉ
CLUNY
E13
MÂCON
Taizé
BROTHER ROGER OF TAIZÉ • B• 1915

BROTHER ROGER OF TAIZÉ

The Church is a kind of sacrament, that is, a sign and instrument of unity, of reconciliation and peace among people, nations, classes and races . . .
The Church becomes more credible if it speaks less about itself and more and more preaches Christ crucified and witnesses to him by its life.

When Brother Roger was 25 years old he left a comfortable life in his native Switzerland to follow a dream. He wanted to found a monastic community devoted to reconciliation. The Second World War was raging when he arrived in a deserted village, Taizé, in Burgundy, France.

Roger bought a house and took in refugees, especially Jews, who were fleeing Nazi occupation. For two years he lived a simple life of poverty, celibacy and prayer. Other young men, inspired by his example, joined him. By Easter 1949 the first small community was established. This has grown steadily and today there are about one hundred Catholic and Protestant brothers in the Taizé community. But the real *community* is much wider. Every week hundreds of young people from all over the world go on pilgrimage to Taizé, to join in the prayer and to reflect on the Gospel.

The Church of Reconciliation is at the heart of a *'city of tents'* where the pilgrims stay. The brothers lead community prayer three times a day. Sometimes the dimly lit building is aglow with candles. Psalms are sung; the Bible is read in different languages followed by a long period of silent prayer. Those who wish stay on and continue praying in song. The Taizé Brothers have composed short chants which are repeated over and over. It is a form of prayer, adapted from eastern traditions, which can lead people deeper into meditation. These chants are now used in churches and schools across the world.

Every Friday evening there are special prayers around the cross to remember all who suffer injustice, poverty or persecution. Brother Roger has always felt concern for those who suffer. He has sent small fraternities of brothers to live amongst the poor in South America, Africa and Asia. When he visits these communities he writes encouraging letters to his brothers at home, returning again and again to his ideal of reconciliation. His most earnest desire is that Christians should lead the way. Taizé, where he asks the brothers to *'live out the parable of community'*, is a proof that Christian denominations can live peacefully together.

What the Scriptures say:

I pray that they may all be one, Father.
John 17:21

Be still and know that I am God.
Psalm 46:10, RSV

Love your enemies and pray for those who persecute you. Matthew 5:44

God, have pity on me, a sinner. Luke 18:13

Jesus, remember me

Music: Jacques Berthier. © Ateliers et Presses de Taizé, 71250, Taizé-Communauté, France

More words from Brother Roger

Never resign yourself to the scandal of the separation of Christians, all so readily professing love for their neighbour, yet remaining divided. Make the unity of Christ's Body your passionate concern.

Love the deprived, all who are suffering injustice and thirsting for justice. Jesus had a special concern for them. Never be afraid of their bothering you.

Youth pilgrimages and retreats

Many young Christians today appreciate the value of silent prayer and pilgrimage. They recognise that Damian Lundy and Anthony Bloom had something important to say when they described prayer as *'going to a rather deeper level than usual'*, and that it is *'born of the discovery that the world has depths'* (see page 13).

This is why thousands of young people go to Taizé each year. Others go to places like Lourdes where they pray and help the sick; and others visit the Scottish island of Iona to join in prayer with a community that also seeks reconciliation.

Church schools set aside time for retreats and reflection days. The sixth-formers in this photograph are at a retreat centre at Kintbury in Berkshire.

The prayer that unites all Christians

Jesus taught his disciples to say:
Our Father, who art in heaven,
hallowed by thy name;
thy kingdom come;
thy will be done on earth as it is in heaven.
Give us this day our daily bread;
and forgive us our trespasses,
as we forgive those who trespass against us;
and lead us not into temptation,
but deliver us from evil. Amen.

Summary

1915 Brother Roger born

1940 Left Switzerland for France – cared for refugees in Taizé

1949 Founded monastic community
Hundreds of young people visit the community every week

Quick questions

1. What was Roger's dream?
2. In what way has he fulfilled it?
3. Describe what it is like in Taizé today.

Longer question

Brother Roger is a monk. In what way is his monastic life different from the life of
(a) a Benedictine monk,
(b) a hermit
(c) a Carmelite nun?

SUMMARY ON PRAYER

Prayer is the raising up of the mind and heart to God. Penny Catechism

Prayer is essentially private and personal because God is best reached when people can *'get in touch with themselves at a deeper level than usual'.* Many people practise meditation. It can lead to contemplation.

Christians, however, often express their personal prayer in a community setting. Vocal prayer (using word formulas) brings the community together. The Church has a liturgical form of prayer that is followed over the year, changing with the pattern of feasts. It is followed in parish churches and in religious communities. This set pattern of prayer centres upon Holy Communion or the Eucharist and is favoured by the Orthodox, Roman Catholic and Anglican Churches. Other churches follow a more informal and free approach to worship.

When Christians meet together they can pray aloud without using formal prayers. In this way they can bring important matters to God which affect each other and the wider world. Some churches have 'prayer meetings' for this purpose.

The five people described in this section have all written about experiences of prayer. Other Christians learn from their example.

GLOSSARY

Anchoress Female hermit. One who chooses a solitary life of prayer

Breviary Prayer book used by priests, monks and nuns. It contains liturgical prayer called the Divine Office

Contemplation Form of prayer without words. Described as *a silent love*

Contemplative Word used to describe monks and nuns who live enclosed in monasteries, devoted to lives of prayer

Lord's Prayer The prayer Jesus taught his disciples. Also known as the *Our Father*

Meditation Using the mind and emotions to reflect on God. Thoughts are often based on Scripture

Mystic One who searches for the most direct experience of God, by concentrating on prayer and fasting

Prayer of the Church Regular pattern of prayer based on set times of prayer, usually prayed in common. Sometimes prayed in public, e.g. Evensong in cathedrals

Vocal prayer The outward expression by voice and gesture of personal prayer. Christians use vocal prayer during their church services

QUESTIONS

(based on examination style questions)

1a. Describe some different forms of prayer.

b. According to the Gospels how and when did Jesus pray?

2. Show how one outstanding Christian followed the example of Jesus and made prayer the focal point of his/her life.

3. 'Nothing really happens when you pray.' Discuss this comment giving different points of view.

SECTION 2: POVERTY

Go and sell all you have . . . give to the poor . . . then come and follow me.

Mark 10:21

Introduction

There are Christians like Sir Cliff Richard who use their wealth to help relieve the poverty of others. Others opt to live in poverty as a way of following Christ. Some choose, like Mother Teresa did, to be poor themselves in order to be at the service of the poor.

In this section we look at four Christians who made poverty the focus of their lives.

Much of Jesus' teaching turns ordinary values upside down. We naturally presume that life should be lived in a certain degree of comfort. We encourage governments to make it possible for everyone to live above a poverty line. We take it for granted that it cannot be good to be poor. Yet Jesus preached: *'Happy are you poor; the Kingdom of God is yours.'* What did he mean?

Jesus was warning people that material wealth could make them feel self-sufficient, and this may blind them to their real dependency on God. There is no record of Jesus handing out money to the poor. He responded to them by giving them a sense of dignity. The Gospels simply portray a man who walked most easily alongside the poor and the neglected. He indicated that it was easier for the poor than for the rich to feel at home in God's Kingdom.

Followers of Jesus recognise that they are completely dependent on God, and that they should be prepared to give up material possessions if they lead to selfishness. They should even give up their own lives if necessary, just as Jesus did. That is the ultimate expression of poverty.

WILLIAM BOOTH

While women weep, as they do now,
I'll fight.
While children go hungry, as they do now,
I'll fight.
While men go to prison, as they do now,
I'll fight.
I'll fight to the very end.

William Booth was born to poor working-class parents in nineteenth-century Nottingham. His father was a builder. When he was only about 15 years old, William experienced a religious conversion: he became a **Methodist** and later a preacher on Tyneside. He married Catherine Mumford in 1855 and together they had a large family. Catherine became a preacher too and was a pioneer in introducing the ministry of women in the Church.

The couple grew impatient with the way in which the traditional Church seemed to ignore the real needs of the poor. There was much poverty in Victorian England. William and Catherine were disturbed by the Gospel texts that described Jesus' preference for the oppressed. They left the Methodist Church in 1862, and suffered isolation and rejection for two years until they began their **Christian Mission** in London's East End. William's direct talk and practical care appealed to ordinary people.

He preached against injustice; especially against child prostitution and slave labour. Then, putting words into practice, he and Catherine began the work for which the **Salvation Army** has become famous. They fed the hungry, clothed the naked, cared for the sick and housed the homeless.

The Salvation Army

In 1878 William Booth established his work on a military model, and the title 'Salvation Army' was adopted two years later. The organisation quickly spread at home and abroad. By the time William died in 1912, his Army had become highly appreciated as a true embodiment of the Gospel.

In today's world, right across the globe whenever there is tragedy, poverty or distress, the Salvation Army officers are in the front line. Their work is persistent and often unsung. In towns and cities the Salvation Army offers practical help to the homeless, to alcoholics, to unmarried mothers, to prisoners, to the anxious and the abandoned. They search for missing persons and care for people living on the street.

Members go out to present the Gospel of Christ as the Good News which overcomes the sin of the world. Music is important in the movement and uniformed brass bands are a familiar sight in the streets. William Booth's question has become famous: *'Why should the devil have all the best tunes?'* Women have enjoyed equal privilege and dignity in the Salvation Army from the beginning. It tends to be run on rather authoritarian lines, but all members, irrespective of status or position, live on a fairly basic wage, just sufficient for ordinary needs.

What the Scriptures say:

The Spirit of the Lord is upon me,
because he has chosen me to bring good news to the poor.
He has sent me to proclaim liberty to the captives
and recovery of sight to the blind;
to set free the oppressed
and announce that the time has come
when the Lord will save his people.

Luke 4:18-19

I was hungry and you fed me,
thirsty and you gave me a drink;
I was a stranger and you received me in your homes,
naked and you clothed me;
I was sick and you took care of me,
in prison and you visited me.

Matthew 25:35-36

Summary

1829 William Booth born
Catherine Mumford born

1844 Converted to Methodism

1855 William married Catherine

1862 They left Methodist Church and preached on the road

1865 London's Christian Mission founded

1878 Reorganised as Salvation Army

1890 Catherine died

1912 William died

Quick questions

1. Why were William and Catherine dissatisfied with traditional churches?
2. Describe the work of the *Christian Mission.*
3. Do you think it is appropriate to base a Christian organisation on the British Army?

WILLIAM BOOTH
B• 1829 D• 1912

FRANCIS OF ASSISI
B. 1181 D. 1226
FLORENCE
AREZZO
GUBBIO
SIENNA
UMBRIA
MONTEPULCIANO
PERUGIA
LAKE
TRASIMENO
ASSISI
ROME

ST FRANCIS OF ASSISI

Feast: 4 October

Go and preach the Gospel, use words if necessary. **Francis**

St Francis was a poet whose whole life was a poem. **G. K. Chesterton**

St Francis is probably the most popular saint of all time. Most people have seen pictures of him as a bearded figure in a rough brown tunic tied with a cord, a bird perched on his shoulder. He is the saint who loved animals and preached with enthusiasm and joy about the Kingdom of God. This comfortable image hides the tough, demanding life that this thirteenth-century Italian led after he chose to follow Jesus' call: *'Go and sell all you have . . . then come and follow me.'*

Francesco Bernardone was the son of a wealthy merchant in Assisi. He had everything – a loving mother, home comforts, good looks and popularity. He led a carefree and careless early life, which included much socialising and even a period as a volunteer knight fighting for his region. When only 20 years old he was taken a prisoner for a year in Perugia after a defeat. This, together with a severe illness, made him think more deeply about his life.

In April 1206 Francis came across a ruined church, San Damiano. There he seemed to hear Jesus speak to him from the cross: *'Francis, rebuild my falling church.'* With enthusiasm he took the words literally and stole some bales of cloth from his father's warehouse to pay for materials to rebuild the little church. His furious father disinherited and disowned him. Francis boldly stripped to the skin in front of his father, gave him back all his rich clothes and, utterly penniless, said he was marrying 'Lady Poverty'.

Some friends joined him and together the twelve poor men decided to base their lives on two Gospel texts (Matthew10:5, 9 and Luke 9:23, see below). By the year 1210, Pope Innocent III recognised the spiritual strength of these young men and authorised them to be roving preachers of Christ, living in utter simplicity and poverty. They lived in huts and walked the paths of central Italy calling people to faith and penitence. They had no set rule of life, owned no property, refused positions in the Church (Francis was never a priest) and lived by accepting any kind of work and gifts of food.

Two years later Francis encouraged his friend Clare to found a community of 'Poor Ladies'. Later he tried to be a missionary among Muslims, but with little success. By 1217 so many men had joined him that the movement began to develop into a religious order. Francis resigned his leadership and eventually retired to Monte La Verna for prayer and solitude. He received the 'Stigmata' – the wounds of Christ on his body. His health deteriorated. He wrote his **Canticle of the Sun** and a final **Testament** before he welcomed 'Sister Death' in 1226.

What the Scriptures say:

These twelve men were sent out by Jesus with the following instructions . . . Do not carry any gold, silver or copper money in your pockets.
Matthew 10:5, 9

If anyone wants to come with me, he must forget self, take up his cross every day, and follow me.
Luke 9:23

St Francis based his Rule for the friars on these two texts.

The Order of Friars Minor today

Francis appealed to the brothers in his final *Testament* to observe absolute poverty, to be obedient to the Rule and to refuse any privileges. But even before he died his idealistic movement began to change. The vast number of brothers required organisation and order. Over the following centuries Franciscans became settled in communities across the world. They were organised, educated, owned property, handled money and some even accepted high positions of authority in the Church. Today Franciscan priests and brothers work in education and in parishes across the world. In Palestine, Roman Catholic Franciscans have been given the custody of the holy places visited by pilgrims.

In 1894 a group of Anglicans who had chosen to follow a Franciscan way of life founded a community in Plaistow, London. The friars looked after the slum dwellers in the East End. Other small groups followed, and between the two Wars the Society of St Francis was founded by Brother Douglas and Father Algy. From its headquarters in Batcombe in Dorset these Anglican Franciscan brothers have spread their work to the United States, Canada, Australia, New Zealand and the Pacific Islands. The brothers work among the most deprived, neglected and outcast people.

Brother Douglas, who died in 1957, was recognised as an English St Francis. He tramped the roads of Britain, sharing the poverty of the homeless, and rescuing the friendless, the depressed and the down-and-outs. He set up shelters to give them breathing space and rest. His work is continued today by his friars and by Anglican sisters.

Ecology

Over the last century world-wide admiration for St Francis has grown amongst Christians and non-Christians alike. Many have been captivated by his single-mindedness, enthusiasm, joyfulness and refusal to be tied down by property and institutions. His written masterpiece, the *Canticle of the Sun*, shows how he identified with the whole of creation, finding God's presence there as the inspiration for his life of poverty.

Canticle of the Sun

O most high, almighty and good Lord God,
To you be praise, glory, honour and blessing.

Praise to you, my Lord, for all your creatures,
especially for Brother Sun
who brings us the day and the light;
how beautiful he is,
and with what splendour he shines.
Praise to you, my Lord, for Sister Moon,
and for the stars so bright in the heavens.
Praise to you, my Lord, for Sister Water,
so precious, so clean, and so humble.
Praise to you, my Lord, for Sister Earth who sustains us and delights us with her many fruits and her coloured flowers and grass.
Praise to you, my Lord, for Sister Death
who will come to embrace each one of us.

Summary

1181 Francesco Bernardone born
1201 Taken prisoner in Perugia
1206 Rebuilt San Damiano church
Disowned by his father
1210 Pope Innocent III sent out the first 12 Friars Minor to preach
1212 Clare founded her community
1219 Francis joined the Crusaders
1222 Retired to Monte La Verna
1224 Wrote *Canticle of the Sun*
1226 He welcomed Sister Death
1228 Made a saint by Pope Gregory IX

Quick questions

1. Why was Francis disowned by his father?
2. Why did Francis turn his back on wealth?
3. Why did Francis and his friends find Matthew 10:5, 9 and Luke 9:23 so appropriate?
4. Write a paragraph about Brother Douglas and Father Algy

Longer questions

Francis has been called the only true Christian in history.

Why do you think this is so?

Would you agree with this statement?

CLARE FEY

Let us try to walk in the Presence of God.
Clare Fey

Even if I had a thousand more sisters we couldn't cope with the need; it would still be a drop in the ocean, so great is the distress and misery of the poor, neglected children.
Andrew Fey

The Industrial Revolution began in Britain in the nineteenth century and then spread across to Europe. Landowners began to take second place to industrialists as machines and manufacturing created a new rich industrial class, along with a new working class crowded into the cities. The immediate result: terrible urban poverty and forced child labour in the factories.

The squalor and suffering in the cities inspired many Christians to action. Several religious congregations were founded at this time. Clare Fey was the foundress of one such group.

Clare's father owned a factory in Aix-La-Chapelle (now called Aachen), an important German city. His family were devout Christians and never lost their commitment to follow the Gospel, especially as they grew more wealthy. Clare's mother encouraged the children to put other people first. When the eldest boy, Andrew, became a priest, he made the family home a meeting place for other priests who were concerned about the unjust distribution of wealth. Clare and her friends attended the meetings. The young women became so determined to help the poor that they overcame the strict nineteenth-century view that women of their background should always stay at home. Anna, Franziska, Pauline, Leokadia and Clare went out into the slums and began to ease the suffering of the most destitute families. Mrs Fey opened a soup kitchen. Then, guided by the energetic and popular Father Andrew, the friends visited the sick and distributed food and clothing.

Mr Fey refused to employ children. Instead Clare and Andrew took them from the streets and began a 'Poor School'. This developed into the founding of a religious order called the 'Congregation of the Poor Child Jesus'. Clare had a way with children, and a calm loving nature. She became the natural leader of the group and inspired everyone by her concern for the poorest children and by her deep sense of prayer. She was to encourage her sisters to 'walk in the presence of God' and to recognise in every poor child the likeness of the poor child Jesus, who was born in poverty and who died in poverty.

What the Scriptures say:

Whenever you did this for one of the least important of these brothers and sisters of mine, you did it for me. Matthew 25:40

Whoever welcomes this child in my name, welcomes me, and whoever welcomes me, also welcomes the one who sent me. Luke 9:48

Sisters of the Poor Child Jesus

When Clare Fey died in 1894, she had seen her foundation grow from a poor school for street children in one city into a world-wide network of schools and homes for orphaned or abused children. Sisters who were not suited to teaching were trained in art and needlework. They became expert in church embroidery, which helped pay for the work with the poor. Clare attracted hundreds of sisters to her congregation, inspired by her quiet determination and her great kindness.

They often worked in hostile conditions and were even the victims of religious persecution. When Germany expelled all religious orders from the country in 1872, Clare had to re-house hundreds of nuns abroad. One group came to England. Over the years the work of the Congregation had to adapt to the changes in society. In Europe, all children now receive free education, and there is less need of children's homes now that fostering and adoption is taken care of by the state. But the traditional work of the sisters continues to be most appropriate in developing countries like Colombia and Indonesia. There the work of Clare Fey's Congregation has long anticipated the Church's more recent call to take an active **Option for the Poor** (see Section 6, page 93).

Religious vocation

Clare and her friends could have lived comfortably, married and had their own families. But they chose to dedicate their whole lives to God in religious life. Anna became a nun in an already established order. Franziska, who had always worked with the adult poor in soup kitchens, founded a congregation called 'Poor Franciscans'. Pauline worked with the blind when her family moved to Paderborn, and she founded the 'Sisters of Christian Charity' to work for the disabled. Clare and Leokadia became the foundation stones of the 'Sisters of the Poor Child Jesus', devoted to caring for and teaching children. The seeds sown in those meetings held in the Fey home had grown into great practical works of charity inspired by the Gospel. The three Congregations still exist, and thousands of young women have followed the example of the five friends.

These **active sisters** take vows of poverty, chastity and obedience to free themselves to work for others, and to enable community life to flourish. Their poverty is not destitution, or even deprivation, but simply the surrender of secular ambitions and possibilities for a life lived under community rules.

Summary

1815 Clare Fey born

1830 Andrew ordained priest

1831 The five friends began work for the poor in Aachen

1837 The Poor School began

1844 Congregation (Sisters) of the Poor Child Jesus founded

1872 Persecution of nuns in Germany

1876 500 PCJ sisters expelled from Germany; some came to England

1894 Clare died

Quick questions

1. How did the Industrial Revolution affect town life?
2. Describe how the Fey family followed their Christian principles.
3. Why did Clare Fey call her congregation Sisters of the Poor Child Jesus?
4. What is a religious vocation?

BOGOTA
COLOMBIA
CLARE FEY
B 1815 D 1894
MEDAN
PATEMBAN
SUMATRA
JAKARTA
JAVA

NANCY
STRASBURG
ALGERIA
MOROCCO
LIBYA
EGYPT
ISRAEL
NAZARETH
CHARLES DE FOUCAULD
B 1858 D 1916

CHARLES DE FOUCAULD

I want to preach the Gospel with my life.

The Little Brother may not have a life apart. He must choose a village, a slum, a nomadic town, settle in it and live as all the others live, especially as the poorest live.

Charles de Foucauld was born into a French Christian family in 1858. Both parents died before he was 6 years old, but loving grandparents gave him a secure childhood. In 1870, war forced his family to move from Strasbourg to Nancy. A difficult time followed, and Charles lost his faith in God. By the age of 16, when he went to study philosophy with the Jesuits in Paris, he had become deeply **agnostic** (unable to say that God exists).

Charles entered the military academy of St Cyr. But the death of his grandfather when he was only 19 was a breaking point. He drifted; he went from one wild party to another; he wasted his inheritance. But he still managed to finish his military training and became an officer, serving in North Africa. He wrote of this time: *'Though I never lost my strong bent for study, in the regiment I went wild. I was far from my family, I hardly saw them between 1878 and 1886, and the little they knew about my life could only have caused them hurt.'*

By 1882 Charles had resigned from the army looking for something more adventurous. He was fascinated with Morocco. He spent the next four years there and in Algeria, returning to Paris in 1886 to publish his account of the dangerous journey. The warm, generous welcome home from family and Christian friends made the young man question his rejection of God. But it was most of all the faith of the Muslims he met that started him on his new search. Later he wrote: *'Islam really shook me to the core. The sight of such faith, of these people living in the continual presence of God, made me glimpse something greater, truer, than worldly concerns. I started studying Islam, and then the Bible.'*

Charles rediscovered God at the age of 28. It was a total conversion and took over his whole life. After a visit to the Holy Land, Charles had found his way: it was to follow Jesus of Nazareth. The poverty and obscurity of Jesus' life in Nazareth shaped his vision. He chose a life of prayer, poverty and manual work. He wanted simply to be there for people around him. The rest of his life took him first to a Trappist monastery, then to Nazareth where he lived in a hut as a servant to a convent of Poor Clares, and finally back as a priest to the desert in North Africa. He chose to live alongside the nomadic Touaregs. He was killed there, in Tamanrasset, Algeria, as the 1914-18 war reached North Africa.

What the Scriptures say:

So Jesus went down with them to Nazareth.
Luke 2:51, RSV

Brother Charles meditated on these words: *'All he did was "go down" his whole life long – he "went down" in the* ***Incarnation****, "went down" in becoming a child, "went down" in becoming poor, abandoned, exiled, persecuted, tortured, in always taking the lowest place.'*

The Little Sisters of Jesus

The humble, quiet life of Brother Charles became an inspiration to others. Young men followed him by leaving academic or worldly positions to hide themselves in obscure and mean places, simply adopting the life of the poor. In 1939, a French woman felt called to adopt a similar life of poverty. **Little Sister Magdeleine** was the first of the Little Sisters of Jesus. She composed a Rule of life based on the example of Brother Charles. He had once written: *'My secret dream is something very simple, very small in numbers, like those first simple communities formed during the earliest days of the Church.'*

The Little Sisters still fulfil that dream. Today there are 1400 Sisters from 60 countries living in small groups across the world. They live with the poor, sharing their living and working conditions in inner cities, in gypsy camps, in rural villages, in shanty towns and in the remote desert. For years Little Sister Magdeleine was treated with suspicion by some Church authorities who said it was 'not worthy' of a religious sister to carry a knapsack, travel like the poor and be nursed in open hospital wards with local people. The advice she gave to her sisters – *'Before being religious, be human and Christian'* – sounded pretty radical in the 1940s.

Today the authorities have recognised that she was right, and her sisters work in factories, as domestics, or in the fields, to support themselves. They say: *'Our life-long call is a non-professional one, a presence of friendship and prayer.'* This friendship extends to all. Brother Charles had written many years before: *'I want all the people who live here, Christians, Muslims, Jews, to get used to thinking of me as their brother, the brother of all.'*

Little Sister Magdeleine

Like Jesus during his life on earth, make yourself 'all things to all people'. Be an Arab in the midst of Arabs, a nomad among nomads, a worker among workers, but above all be human. Do not think that living among people will hinder your life of union with God. Do not think that as a religious you have a special dignity to safeguard.

Little Sister Magdeleine, to her sisters

Summary

1858 Charles de Foucauld born

1876 Military training

1878 Service in N. Africa

1882 He resigned

1883 Went to Algeria and Morocco

1886 Conversion

1890 Joined Trappist Monastery

1897 Left for Nazareth

1901 Ordained priest. Went to Algeria

1916 Killed in Tamanrasset

Quick questions

1. Show how Nazareth became the inspiration for Brother Charles' life.
2. Describe the lives of the Little Sisters of Jesus.
3. Why were Church authorities unhappy with their style of life?
4. Do you think it is better to live like the poor *or* help the poor to live like you?

LITTLE SISTER
MAGDELEINE
B·1898 - D·1989

SUMMARY ON POVERTY

Poverty in the Gospel is a paradox. On the one hand Jesus inspires people to help others out of their poverty; yet on the other hand he warns people about the dangers of comfort and wealth. He suggests it is good to be poor.

1. There are many saints and good people who, over the centuries, have devoted their lives and wealth to helping others. Clare Fey is one example of those who chose to work amongst the poor at great personal cost.

2. There are others, like Francis and Charles de Foucauld, who took Jesus' words literally when he said: *'Don't be always concerned about what you will eat and drink . . . Your Father knows you need these things, and he will provide you with them'* (Luke 12:29-31). They and their followers chose to be absolutely free from material goods so they were in no danger of *'storing up riches on earth'* (Matthew 6:19). Jesus had warned: *'Your heart will always be where your riches are'* (Matthew 6:21).

All Christians are invited to be dependent on God, not on material things.

GLOSSARY

Active sisters Religious sisters who do various forms of charitable work outside the convent

Agnostic One who believes that nothing can be known of God's existence

Canticle of the Sun The poem written by St Francis of Assisi

Christian Mission The first foundation made by William Booth in London's East End

Friars Minor The 'lesser' friars, the name given to followers of St Francis

Incarnation Means 'in the body'. Christians believe that the mystery of God is embodied in the man Jesus

Methodists The followers of John Wesley

Nazareth The insignificant town where Jesus grew up

Option for the Poor A definitive move made recently by the Catholic Church to put the needs of the poor first

Religious vocation The call to a way of living the Gospel in communities of prayer and good works

Salvation Army The organisation founded by William Booth

Testament The last advice given by St Francis to his friars

QUESTIONS

1. Read the story of the RICH YOUNG MAN (Mark 10:17-31).
   (a) Rewrite this in your own words (no more than 100).
   (b) Does Jesus say it is wrong to own money and goods?
   (c) Describe the life of one person who left everything to follow Jesus.

2. Read the parable of the GREAT FEAST (Luke 14:15-24).
   (a) Rewrite it in your own words (no more than 100).
   (b) What does the parable suggest about the dangers of wealth?
   (c) Discuss the following statement: The demands Jesus makes on his disciples to be poor are quite impossible.

SECTION 3: TEACHING

Go, then, to all peoples everywhere
and make them my disciples.

Matthew 28:19

Introduction

Teaching has always been a vital element in the life of the Church. In this section we look at four different teachers, two of them Gospel writers, a theologian and a preacher.

Without the Evangelists we could not know Jesus. They rooted the reality of his life in history for us. Of the four accounts of the life and teaching of Jesus, those by Mark, Matthew and Luke have some similarities. They are called the **Synoptic** ('look alike') Gospels. John, who wrote later, used a different style, more meditative and reflective.

It is thought that Mark wrote first (after AD 65), followed by Matthew, about ten years later. Luke then wrote his account after AD 85. It is important to realise that the Gospels are statements of faith, *not* biographies. Even so, real events are described in their pages, and no one doubts that Jesus was in fact a healer and controversial Jewish preacher. His views were unacceptable to the religious authorities and were punished by the death penalty. The extraordinary event three days later puts the Gospel writing into context. It must be read in the light of the resurrection.

Matthew and the other Evangelists wrote their Gospels as proclamations of *faith*. They believed Jesus was the Messiah, the Son of God. They wrote to share this belief with other disciples, then and now.

ST MATTHEW

Feast: 21 September

Every teacher of the Law who becomes a disciple in the Kingdom of Heaven is like the owner of a house who takes new and old things out of his storeroom.

Matthew 13:52

(This is possibly a description of himself.)

Who was Matthew? For many centuries it was presumed that the author of the longest Gospel was Matthew Levi, otherwise known as Matthew the tax collector, who became an apostle. But nothing is really known about him, apart from evidence found in the text.

Some recent scholars suggest that it is more likely that a former scribe (teacher of the Law), wrote this Gospel. It was written ten years or so after Mark, using much of Mark's material. Why would it do that if the writer had been an apostle? Surely the author would not have needed to copy someone else's stories about Jesus. Even so, there are some original stories in this Gospel, and it is possible that these came from the Apostle Matthew's memory, so his name was given to the whole writing.

The entire work is clearly written by a Jewish follower of Jesus and it is addressed to all those with a Jewish background. It has the tone of a teacher and such familiarity with Jewish Scripture as only a scribe would have at his fingertips. Whoever this Matthew was, he has given to Christianity a picture of Jesus as *the* great teacher. The author's own skill as a teacher lies in the richness of his text.

The kerygma

The first preached message about Jesus by the early disciples was known as the **kerygma** (Greek). Peter and Paul, for example, proclaimed their faith in Jesus and preached to the crowds. This is recorded in the *Acts of the Apostles*.

Summary of the kerygma

All history has come to fulfilment.
The life of Jesus showed him to be the Messiah promised in the Jewish Scriptures.

- He died as God had foretold.
- God raised him from the dead and placed him at his right hand.
- He will save those who accept him as saviour.
- Repent and be baptised.

The sources in Matthew's Gospel

These are not altogether clear, but biblical scholars have made some suggestions.

1. Matthew relied on Mark's Gospel written some ten years earlier, and copied most of it. (Mark was based on the kerygma.)
2. He added long *discourses*. Luke has some of these in his Gospel and he may have copied Matthew. But the common opinion is that Matthew and Luke used another document, written by earlier disciples. This document is now lost, and is known as 'Q'.
3. The Gospel of Matthew has about 300 verses not found anywhere else. They are known as 'M'. Matthew, the tax collector, may have provided these.

What is special about the Gospel of Matthew, the teacher evangelist?

Matthew invites his readers to understand Jesus in the way he understood him. He was convinced that all the Jewish hopes had been fulfilled in Jesus. He took texts and ideas from the Jewish Scriptures (we call this the Old Testament) and interwove them into the life of Jesus. He saw Jesus as the new Moses.

Rooted in his Jewish background, Matthew understood that the People of God could be best understood in terms of

- Moses and the Law;
- the Prophets who continued the work of Moses;
- the Liberator promised to Moses.

Matthew saw Jesus against this backdrop. The heart of Matthew's Gospel is arranged around five great discourses, for he presents Jesus as the great Teacher who has the authority to interpret the Law of God. Those who accepted Jesus' teaching were the new People of God.

Summary

Matthew rewrote Mark's Gospel

He added new material

He wrote about AD 75

He had an educated Jewish background

He wrote for Palestinian Jews who had become Christians

He saw Jesus as the great Teacher

Jesus appears as the new Moses

The Jewish style is poetic and repetitious

Quick questions

1. What is the kerygma?
2. Who was Matthew?
3. Show how Matthew's Gospel is written against a backdrop of Judaism.

MATTHEW • FIRST CENTURY •

1 The book of the generation of Jesus Christ, the son of David,[1] the son of Abraham.[2]
2 Abraham begat Isaac; and Isaac begat Jacob; and Jacob begat Judas and his brethren;
3 And Judas begat Phares and Zara of Thamar; and Phares begat Esrom; and Esrom begat Aram;
4 And Aram begat Aminadab; and Aminadab begat Naasson; and Naasson begat Salmon;
5 And Salmon begat Booz of Rachab; and Booz begat Obed of Ruth; and Obed begat Jesse;
6 And Jesse begat David the king; and David the king begat Solomon of her *that ha*
7 And Solomon beg ... Abia; and Abia begat Asa;
8 And Asa be ... ; and Joram begat
9 And Ozia ... ; and Achaz be
10 And Ez ... and Am
11 And Jo ... they we
12 And a ... Salathi
13 And Z ... and Eli
14 And

מתתיהו

זה ספר תולדת המשיח ישוע בן־דוד בן־אברהם:
אברהם הוליד את־יצחק ויצחק הוליד את־יעקב
3 ויעקב הוליד את־יהודה ואת־אחיו: ויהודה הוליד
את־פרץ ואת־זרח מתמר ופרץ הוליד את־חצרון
וחצרון הוליד את־רם: ורם הוליד את־עמינדב
ועמינדב הוליד את־נחשון ונחשון הוליד את־שלמון:
5 ושלמון הוליד את־בעז מרחב ובעז הוליד את־עובד
6 מרות ועובד הוליד את־ישי: וישי הוליד את־המלך
דוד ודוד הוליד את־שלמה מהאשה אשר לקח
7 מאוריה: ושלמה הוליד את־רחבעם ורחבעם הוליד
8 את־אביה ואביה הוליד את־אסא: ואסא הוליד
את־יהושפט ויהושפט הוליד את־יהורם ויהורם
9 הוליד את־עזיהו: ועזיהו הוליד את־יותם ויותם
10 הוליד את־אחז ואחז הוליד את־חזקיהו: וחזקיהו
הוליד את־מנשה ומנשה הוליד את־אמון ואמון
11 הוליד את־יאשיהו: ויאשיהו הוליד את־יכניהו ואת־
אחיו בימי גלותם בבלה:
12 ואחרי הגלם לבבל יכניהו הוליד את־שאלתיאל
13 ושאלתיאל הוליד את־זרבבל: וזרבבל הוליד את־
אביהוד ואביהוד הוליד את־אליקים ואליקים הוליד
14 את־עזור: ועזור הוליד את־צדוק וצדוק הוליד את־
15 יכין ויכין הוליד את־אליהוד: ואליהוד הוליד את־
אלעזור

ΚΑΤΑ ΛΟΥΚΑΝ 23, 24

ἰδὼν δὲ ὁ ἑκατοντάρχης τὸ γενόμενον 47
ἐδόξαζεν τὸν Θεὸν λέγων·
Ὄντως ὁ ἄνθρωπος οὗτος δίκαιος ἦν.

Literal Translation (H.J.R. 1999)

The commander-of-a-hundred,
seeing what had happened,
praised God saying:
"Truly this was a good man."

New English Bible

The centurion saw it all,
and gave praise to God.
"Beyond all doubt", he said,
"This man was innocent."

New World Bible

The officer in charge of the guard
was watching.
"This man was innocent," he said.

Authorised Version

Now when the centurion
saw what was done,
he glorified God, saying,
"Certainly this was a righteous man."

Jerusalem Bible

When the centurion saw
what had taken place,
he gave praise to God and said,
"Truly this was an upright man."

ST LUKE

Feast: 18 October

> ***Dear Theophilus,***
> ***In my first book, I wrote about all the things that Jesus did and taught from the time he began his work until the day he was taken up to heaven.***
> **Luke, in Acts of the Apostles 1:1-2**

Who was Luke? He was a Gentile (non-Jewish) doctor, an educated man. He may have become a disciple of Jesus through his friend, Paul. We know from Paul's letters that he took Luke with him on some of his missionary journeys. It seems unlikely that he ever met Jesus, so he did not write as an eyewitness.

Luke was a good Greek scholar. He wrote over one quarter of the New Testament: his *Gospel* and the *Acts of the Apostles*. All his writing was thorough, careful and very well researched. His style is sometimes formal and sometimes poetic. Like all Greeks, Luke had a tidy mind. He liked things in order, so he mentions places, people and dates; he was concerned to put Jesus in a proper historical context.

It is clear that Luke warmed to Jesus' compassion. Perhaps being a medical doctor, Luke could closely identify with the day-to-day sufferings of ordinary people. He presents Jesus as a compassionate man whose concern was for the poor, the outcasts, and people whose lives were a mess. Luke showed how Jesus' attitude towards women was unique. He treated them as equals – unheard of in that time and culture. Luke could understand Jesus.

Luke wrote his Gospel some time after AD 85, about ten years after Matthew's Gospel. He addresses a much wider readership, because he wrote for both Jews and Gentiles. His message was that the Good News was for *everyone*. Luke had a great dream for the future, where love would break down all barriers of race and culture.

Luke's is the happiest of Gospels, which suggests that he was himself a contented and joyful person. The angel's message in his opening pages sums up the whole Gospel: *'I am here with good news for you, which will bring great joy to all the people'* (Luke 2:10).

The sources Luke used

Luke assured his readers that he researched his work and gathered all available material before he started. He told Theophilus (to whom he addresses his writings), *'I thought it would be good to write an orderly account for you'* (Luke 1:3).
He based his work:

(1) on Mark
(2) on Matthew
(3) on the lost document, known as 'Q'
(4) on his own material – Luke proper – which makes up one quarter of the Gospel.

Teaching in parables

Luke was deeply impressed by the effect Jesus had on his disciples, so impressed that he believed Jesus was indeed the Son of God, and that he had brought the Kingdom of God into our midst. Matthew had presented Jesus as the great Teacher, in the style of Moses. Luke presented Jesus as a teacher, too. But he presented him as the Jewish rabbi, who used stories to make people sit up and think.

Jesus wanted to give glory to God, his Father. When he began preaching it was to teach about God's Kingdom. He told stories, **parables**, to describe this Kingdom. It is Luke who loves to retell these stories. He has thirty-five parables telling what God's Way is like.

> *'The Kingdom of God is like this. A woman takes some yeast and mixes it with forty litres of flour until the whole batch of dough rises.'*
> Luke 13:20

Luke has another twenty-two parables telling what those unprepared for the Kingdom are like. He records many more parables than the other evangelists, and is the only one to record the best-known of these stories: the Good Samaritan and the Lost (Prodigal) Son.

Luke, the humanitarian

Luke is sometimes called the first humanitarian. This is because Jesus, in Luke's Gospel, is most at home with ordinary people. He seems to prefer the poor and the outcasts, though he addresses everyone. Women and children gather round him to listen to his teaching of love and forgiveness. Luke also portrayed a human, exhausted Jesus, needing again and again to withdraw from the crowds to regain his strength in prayer.

Summary

Luke re-edited the Gospels of Mark and Matthew

He added new material

He wrote after AD 85

He was a highly educated Greek doctor

He wrote for Jews and Gentiles

He presented Jesus' enormous concern for the poor and outcasts

He shows Jesus as the rabbi, teller of stories (parables)

The Gospel is orderly, and put into its historical context

Quick questions

1. Who was Luke?
2. Why is he called the *first great humanitarian*?
3. Look up the following texts:
   (1) Luke 10:25-37
   (2) Luke 15:11-32
   Retell both parables in your own words, and explain them.

ST THOMAS AQUINAS

Feast: 7 March

> ***His wonderful learning owes far less to his genius than to the effectiveness of his prayer.***
> **The Dominicans**

In every century there have been great thinkers who seek for clearer understanding of the Bible and of the Church's teaching (or doctrine). One of the greatest thinkers, known as **theologians**, was Thomas Aquinas.

Thomas was born in Italy, at Roccasecca, in AD 1225. He was one of many children of Landulf, a rich nobleman, and was educated by the Benedictines at Monte Cassino. Later, as an undergraduate at the University of Naples, Thomas joined the Dominicans, an order of highly educated mendicant (begging) friars. His relatives were absolutely shocked for he was only 19 years old and from a noble family: the friars lived in considerable poverty. Thomas' brothers kidnapped him and shut him away for a year, but this did not make him change his mind. Eventually he continued his theological studies as a Dominican, in Paris and Cologne.

Thomas returned to Paris to teach. He later taught in Naples and other Italian cities. But he is best known for his extraordinarily large output of writings. These philosophical and theological works have had enormous influence on the Church. In 1879 his works were recognised by Pope Leo XIII as the very basis of Catholic teaching.

1. Between 1259 and 1264 he wrote **Summa Contra Gentiles**. In this work about God and creation he argues that reason and faith are in perfect harmony with each other.
2. Between 1266 and 1273 he wrote his twenty-two volume **Summa Theologica**. This was a complete exposition of theology covering the nature of God and our relationship with him, morality and the work of Jesus. He left it unfinished.

Thomas explored and expressed Christian revelation using the philosophical ideas of Aristotle, which was a bold thing to do at that time. Of course his work embodied a medieval world view, but the substance of his thinking continues to be highly respected.

Thomas was only 49 years old when he died whilst on his way to take part in a Church Council at Lyons. He was canonised (made a saint) only fifty years later. The Dominicans call him the Angelic Doctor because he was, first and foremost, a man of prayer.

What the Scriptures say:

> *What you have heard in private you must announce from the housetops.* Matthew 10:27
>
> *Whoever listens to you listens to me.*
> Luke 10:16

The Dominican Order of Preachers

Dominic Guzman was born in Castile in 1170, just eleven years before St Francis of Assisi (see page 31). He was a keen student at the University of Palencia until, aged 24, he became a priest of the Reformed Canons Regular. Like Francis he was full of zeal for the poor and the suffering: *'He bore their affliction in the close sanctuary of his compassion and tears'* (his first biographer, Jordan of Saxony).

In 1205 Dominic went with his bishop, Diego, to Rome, to ask Pope Innocent III's permission to start a foreign mission. However, the pope was at this time more concerned about the Albigensian **heretics**. They were teaching that everything material was from the devil (marriage, for example, was evil!) This heresy needed to be countered by a strong force of enthusiastic and inspiring men. Pope Innocent therefore persuaded Diego and Dominic to accept a preaching mission in the South of France, where he had already sent Cistercian monks to combat the heretics. Dominic's enthusiasm looked highly promising.

Despite great difficulties Dominic preached the Gospel for six years, almost alone. (He loved St Matthew's Gospel.) By 1215 he had been joined by six companions and the Order of Friars Preachers was born. The group increased very quickly as a number of highly educated theologians joined the new foundation, all distinctly dressed in black. Dominic was soon able to send his 'Blackfriars' across Europe, and some even came to Oxford. He travelled around Europe on foot to visit them all. He died in 1221, aged only 50 years, and was canonised a few years later, when young Thomas Aquinas was just 8 years old.

Today we know the Order of Friars Preachers as **Dominicans** and they remain a strong force in the Church.

Summary

1170 Dominic Guzman born

1215 Order of Friars Preachers founded

1221 Dominic died

1225 Thomas Aquinas born

1244 Thomas became a Preaching Friar

1264 He completed *Summa Contra Gentiles*

1273 He stopped writing the *Summa Theologica*

1274 Thomas died

Quick questions

1. Write a short account of the life of St Dominic and the Order he founded.
2. Why is Thomas Aquinas so important in the Church?
3. Compare the lives of St Francis (page 31) and St Dominic.

THOMAS
AQUINAS
B•1225 • D•1274
SUMMA
THEOLOGICA

GALICIA
ASTURIAS
LEON
NAVARRE
BURGOS
CATALONIA
ZARAGOZA
ARAGON
SALAMANCA
AREVALO
SEGOVIA
ALCALA
MADRID
CASTILLE
TOLEDO
VALENCIA
CORDOBA
GRANADA
DOMINIC GUZMAN
B·1170 · D·1221

JOHN WESLEY

I look upon all the world as my parish.

I never undertake any more work than I can get through in perfect calmness of spirit.

In the early eighteenth century the Anglican rector of Epworth and his wife became the proud parents of two sons: John, followed by Charles. The Wesley brothers were to have a remarkable influence on Christianity in England.

John was a keen student and went to Christ Church College, Oxford, when just 17. He was ordained a priest in the Church of England and for a short spell assisted his father in Lincolnshire. In 1729 he returned to Oxford as a tutor. By this time Charles was studying at Christ Church College and his circle of friends had become known as the *Holy Club* or the *Oxford Methodists*, because they were so exact about following their religious practices. John joined the group.

In 1735, after their father's death, the brothers went to Georgia, USA, as missionaries, but were unsuccessful. Their enthusiasm probably went over the top because they aroused only hostility. Three years later, on returning to England, John met with similar angry reactions when, converted to an evangelical faith in Christ, he began to preach about salvation with extraordinary zeal. The comfortable parish clergy were not used to such enthusiasm and disturbance and closed their pulpits to him.

Undaunted, John took to the road and began to preach in the open air. He took the Gospel (Good News) out to the people, rather as Jesus had done. In Bristol he founded his first chapel. He was joined by brother Charles, and they adopted the name '**Methodist**'. From being rigidly **High Church of England** the brothers became **Evangelical** Christians.

For the next fifty years John roamed the countryside on horseback, addressing crowds of working people: miners, foundry-men, farmers, weavers and casual town workers. Sometimes crowds of over 20,000 would wait patiently for hours to hear a Wesley sermon. By the time of his death in 1791, John had an enormous following. He had founded many Methodist chapels across the country, written numerous scholarly works and biographies, and published his sermons. These were so popular that he earned thousands of pounds which he gave away to charity. The sermons also became the guidelines for the teaching of the Methodist Church.

John was always reluctant to form a Church of his own, and struggled desperately to remain within the Church of England. But after his death the tension had become too great and the split came. Today there are over fifty million Methodists worldwide.

What the Scriptures say:

Go and preach, 'The Kingdom of Heaven is near!' Matthew 10:7

We cannot stop speaking of what we ourselves have seen and heard. Acts 4:20

What the Churches say:

To evangelise is to spread the good news that Jesus Christ died for our sins and was raised from the dead according to the Scriptures, and that as the reigning Lord he now offers the forgiveness of sins and the liberating gift of the Spirit to all who repent and believe.

The Lausanne Covenant

Charles Wesley

Charles was four years younger than John. He remained in his older brother's shadow, yet faithfully supported him throughout his life. He is, however, better remembered than John because he was the greatest hymn writer of the eighteenth century. He wrote over 5,500 hymns, many of them recognised as being of the highest quality. They are sung universally across the Christian denominations. Among the best known are *Hark, the herald angels sing* and *Love divine, all loves excelling.*

Love divine, all loves excelling,
joy of heaven, to earth come down;
fix in us thy humble dwelling,
all thy faithful mercies crown:
Jesu, thou art all compassion,
pure, unbounded love thou art;
visit us with thy salvation,
enter every trembling heart.

The Evangelical Movement

Another enthusiastic religious group sprang up in the nineteenth century, and became known as the **Evangelical Movement**. It was associated with the Reverend Charles Simeon (died 1836). He wanted to raise fervour and higher ethical standards amongst the Church of England clergy. The teaching of the movement was based on the message of the Gospels.

The members had a strong social conscience and supported William Wilberforce in his campaign against the slave trade. They worked to improve the living conditions of the poor. Associated with the Evangelical Movement was the religious education provided by the Bible Society, founded a few years earlier.

Summary

1703 John Wesley born

1707 Charles Wesley born

1729 Both brothers in Oxford, known as the Oxford Methodists

1735 Unsuccessful missionary journey to America

1738 John refused pulpits in the Church of England. Began to preach in the open

1739 Methodist movement grew

1788 Charles died

1791 John died

Quick questions

1. Write a brief biography of John Wesley.
2. Why were the group called 'Methodists'?
3. Write a brief biography of Charles Wesley.
4. What is the Evangelical Movement?

CHARLESTON
ATLANTA
SAVANNAH
NEW ORLEANS
JACKSONVILLE
ORLANDO
MIAMI
JOHN WESLEY B· 1703 · D· 1791

A charge to keep I have
All thanks be to God
All ye that pass by
And are we yet alive
And can it be that I should gain
Behold the Lamb of God
Blest be the dear uniting love
Blow ye the trumpet, blow
Christ the Lord is risen today
Christ, from whom all blessings flow
Christ, whose glory fills the skies
Come, and let us join our friends above
Come, and let us sweetly join
Come, Divine Interpreter
Come, holy and celestial Dove
Come, Holy Ghost, all quickenin[illegible]
Come, Holy Ghost, our hearts [illegible]
Come, let us use the grace divi[illegible]
Come, let us who in Christ bel[illegible]
Come, O thou all victorious L[illegible]
Come, O thou traveller unkn[illegible]
Come, sinners to the Gospel f[illegible]
Come, thou long expected Je[illegible]
Depth of mercy! Can there b[illegible]
Earth, rejoice, our Lord is king
Entered the holy place above
Father of all, in whom alone
Father, in whom we live
Forth in thy name, O Lord
Glory be to God on high
God is gone up on high
God of unexampled grace
Good thou art, and good thou d[illegible]
Granted is the Sa[illegible]r's prayer
Hail the day th[illegible]im rise
Happy the man th[illegible]ds the grac[illegible]
Hark! The herald an[illegible] sing
How can we sinners know
How shall a s[illegible]
I want a prin[illegible]
I want the spirit of power within
Infinite God, [illegible]raise our hearts
Jesu, lover of my soul
Jesu, the word[illegible]
Jesus comes with all his grace
Jesus to thee we fly
Jesus! The name high over all
Jesus, if still the same thou art
Jesus, in whom the weary find
Jesus, Lord, we look to thee
Jesus, the conqueror, reigns
Jesus, the first and last
Jesus, the sinner's friend, to thee
Jesus, thine all-victorious love
Jesus, thy far extended fame
Jesus, united by thy grace

Jesus, we on the word depend
Lamb of God, whose dying love
Let earth and heaven agree
Let earth and heaven combine
Let us plead for faith alone
Light of those whose dreary dwelling
Lo, he comes with clouds descending
Lord, we believe to us and ours
Love divine, all loves excelling
Maker, in whom we live
Mee[illegible]right it is to sing
My h[illegible]ull of Christ
No[illegible]hurun's God
O [illegible]ll in me
O [illegible]rs, to your Lord
O [illegible]
O for [illegible]aise my God
O for a th[illegible]ngues to sing
[illegible]
[illegible]look down from above
O Jesus [illegible]
O Jesus, f[illegible] and grace
O [illegible]ve [illegible] hast thou done
O thou [illegible] from above
O thou [illegible]e they flocked to hear
[illegible]mer
[illegible]rom the dead
Pra[illegible] reigns above
[illegible]ng
[illegible]
Sa[illegible] of Israel[illegible]race
Sa[illegible] we know thou art
See[illegible] great a flame aspires
Sin[illegible]rs, turn; why will ye die?
So[illegible]iers of Christ, arise
Sp[illegible]t of Faith, come down
S[illegible]endous height of heavenly love
[illegible] will I praise with all my heart
[illegible] hidden source of calm repose
[illegible]easeless, unexhausted love
[illegible] faithfulness, Lord, each moment we find
[illegible]finished! The Messiah dies
To us a child of royal birth
We know by faith, we surely know
Weary souls that wander wide
What shall I do, my God, to love
When quiet in my house I sit
When shall thy love constrain
Where shall my wondering soul begin?
Wherewith, O God, shall I draw near
With glorious clouds encompassed round
Would Jesus have the sinner die?
Ye faithful souls whom Jesus know
Ye neighbours and friends of Jesus draw near
Ye servants of God

SUMMARY ON TEACHING

Jesus was a good teacher. He made people sit up and listen. Like most easterners he loved using stories (parables). His teaching was about God's Kingdom. He identified those who were already in the Kingdom – the compassionate, the forgiving, the generous, and the loving.

Jesus practised what he preached. In fact, disciples learn as much from his example as from his words. Over the centuries many Christians have passed on Jesus' message, some by example and some by teaching.

The four evangelists were the first great Christian teachers. Thomas Aquinas is a giant amongst teachers of the Faith. He taught through his writings. John Wesley was a great Christian who taught through the spoken word when he addressed crowds around the country.

GLOSSARY

Dominicans	Order of Preachers founded by Saint Dominic
Evangelical Christians	Protestants who emphasise the authority of the Bible, faith and a 'born again' personal commitment
Heretics	Those who pick and choose their beliefs, so separating themselves from the wider community of the Church
High Church of England	The branch of the Anglican Church stressing continuity with Catholic Christianity
Kerygma	The first preached message about Jesus by early disciples
Methodists	Followers of John Wesley. They split from the Church of England after his death (eighteenth century)
Parables	Striking stories Jesus used to describe the Kingdom of God
Synoptic	The three Gospels that have similarities (look alike): Mark, Matthew and Luke
Summa Contra Gentiles	Work of Thomas Aquinas where he argues that reason and faith are compatible
Summa Theologica	Twenty-two volumes by Thomas Aquinas on the nature of God and our relationship with him
Theologians	Scholars who study and explore ideas about God

QUESTIONS

1. What is known about (a) Matthew the Evangelist and (b) Luke the Evangelist?
2. (a) The Gospels are not biographies. What are they?

   (b) Describe the differences between Matthew's Gospel and Luke's.
3. Much of the Church's teaching (doctrine) was formulated by St Thomas Aquinas in the thirteenth century. Some say that this means it must be outdated. Others say that he described the **truth** which cannot change.

   What do you think? Give reasons for your answer.
4. Two Christians disagree with each other. One says: *'I do not need a Church. I follow the Gospels.'* The other says: *'I need my Christian community. I am part of the Body of Christ.'*

   Write a conversation between the two, developing both arguments.

PARIS
MARSEILLES
ROME
MADRID
VINCENT DE PAUL
B. 1580 • D. 1660

SECTION 4: HEALING

Jesus healed many who were sick with all kinds of diseases.

Mark 1:34

Introduction

Healing means more than just making physically well. The people we look at in this section were concerned, like Jesus, that people should be 'whole': healed physically, mentally, emotionally and spiritually.

It is very clear from the Gospels that Jesus worked miracles of healing. Miracles are important to the evangelists as they bear witness to the power of God working through Jesus. It is not easy to identify what exactly took place at the time. But one consistent picture of Jesus emerges – he was full of compassion for people sick in mind and body.

Luke, the doctor, is most in sympathy with this aspect of Jesus' character. He records many instances where Jesus reached out to people on the edge of society – lepers, social outcasts, the poor, the dispossessed. Christians have always been influenced by this example. Early monastic communities looked after the sick. In later centuries countless religious orders, like the Vincentians, were founded in response to poverty, suffering and oppression.

Outstanding Christians like Mother Teresa and Dame Cicely Saunders have been inspired by Jesus to dedicate their lives to healing. Countless unnamed Christians, worldwide, follow this same path.

ST VINCENT DE PAUL

Feast: 27 September

There was no human suffering that he did not seek to relieve . . . and his single-minded goodness and generosity stirred a like generosity in others.

Donald Attwater

In seventeenth-century France, both politics and religion were in chaos. It needed someone extraordinary to turn things around. That someone was Vincent de Paul, a lively and energetic man, born in humble circumstances in Gascony in the South of France. He was eventually to dominate life in Paris, in the courts of kings and cardinals. He convinced noblemen and women to work for the poor and the sick. He persuaded the worldly and selfish clergy to reform their lives. And he became the bridge builder between social classes, between Protestants and Catholics, and between politicians and Church leaders.

Vincent was not always so unselfish. As a young man he was ambitious and adventurous. His father had to sell some of the family farm to pay for Vincent's studies in Toulouse, after which he entered the priesthood. After ordination, he was left some money in a will, but was cheated of it, and scoured the Mediterranean in search of the embezzler. On the high seas he was captured by pirates, and sold as a slave to a Turkish alchemist in North Africa. He escaped and met up with an influential Italian priest who introduced him to the Papal court in Rome. From there he was sent to the court of King Henry IV in Paris. At this point, Vincent could have settled for a life of comfort.

But the young priest found he was living in two contrasting worlds, the privilege of the few and the poverty of the rest. The Queen, Margot of Valois, appointed Vincent her chaplain and adviser, and took him to see her charitable works – the hospitals in Paris. There he saw the sick, the dying and the dead, all huddled together in squalor. Shocked, Vincent was tempted to retire to a simple parish near his family, but a meeting with Peter de Berulle changed his life. Peter de Berulle told him to look at God, not at himself.

Vincent was transformed. He became consumed with concern for the poor and with a determination to heal the wounds of the Paris in which he lived, with its family feuds, religious prejudice and scandalously degenerate clergy. He found he had a great talent for organisation. After

Mass he would send his parishioners to visit the sick and take gifts to the poor. He used his influence in the royal and noble courts to initiate 'meals on wheels', famine relief, child-care schemes and hospital visitors. To help him in this work, he founded two religious orders to spread these activities throughout France and beyond.

After forty years of organisation, reformation and supervision of his religious foundations, Vincent spent his old age writing to his sisters and brother priests. He encouraged, comforted, admonished and praised them. Over 4,000 of his letters have been kept. They bear witness to his humble and saintly humanity.

The Vincentian Communities

St Vincent de Paul was a great social worker. But his organisational genius and his great compassion were rooted in faith in Jesus. He believed that both rich and poor were called to be part of the Kingdom of God. That came first. To help in this mission he founded two religious congregations.

Vincent founded his first religious order in 1625 when he was working for the poor tenants on the estates of General Philip and Madame de Gondi, where he enlisted the help of sympathetic priests. He called these priests the Congregation of the Mission, and sent them to preach the Gospel to the poor and to the rich. He urged them to give priority to people's religious needs, whilst not forgetting their human poverty. The Congregation grew over the years, and is today known in England as the **Vincentians**. These priests are engaged in education, retreat work, social work and missions abroad. Their most well-known foundation in England is St Mary's College for teacher training in Twickenham.

In 1628 Vincent was helped in the running of his charities by a widow, Mademoiselle le Gras, known today as **St Louise de Marillac**. She and Vincent were joint founders of the **Daughters of Charity**. This religious institution was revolutionary in the Church. They had 'no monastery but the sick room, no cell but the hired lodging, no chapel but the parish church and no cloister but the street'. Many young women joined the group, and by the time Vincent died the sisters were running most of the hospitals and orphanages in France, and in countries as far away as Poland. Today the Daughters of Charity (now known as Sisters of Charity) are a very large religious community, running hospitals, schools for the blind and the deaf, homes for the aged and hostels for the homeless.

The Society of Vincent de Paul

Two hundred years later, in 1830, a group of university students in war-torn Paris felt they should do something to help their neighbours. Led by Frederick Ozanam, they decided to follow the example of St Vincent de Paul. Their work grew into a large organisation. In parish groups, called 'conferences', young and older parish members offer all kinds of help to those in need – from visiting hospitals and prisons to running clubs, distributing goods to struggling families and decorating homes for the elderly. Some schools have SVP conferences and keep in touch with each other through their newspaper, the *Young Vincentian*.

What the Scriptures say:

The Lord chose another seventy-two men and sent them out two by two . . . He said to them . . . 'Whenever you go into a town and are made welcome, eat what is set before you, heal the sick in that town, and say to the people there, "The Kingdom of God has come near you".'

Luke 10:1, 8-9

Summary

1580 Vincent de Paul born

1600 Ordained priest

1609 Joined Royal Court in Paris

1625 Founded Congregation of the Mission

1628 Founded Daughters of Charity
Work expanded across the world

1660 Vincent died

1830 Students founded the **SVP Society**

Quick questions

1. St Vincent de Paul has been called 'Champion of the Poor.' Explain why.
2. Describe the two religious foundations established by St Vincent de Paul.
3. Describe the organisation founded in Paris in 1830.

LOUISE
DE MARILLAC
B• 1591 • D• 1660

ALBERT SCHWEITZER
B • 1875 • D • 1965
415
E9
417
COLMAR
MUNSTER
GABON
LAMBARENE

ALBERT SCHWEITZER

Schweitzer came to survey his happiness and to wonder if it were right for him to accept it unthinkingly. On the one hand there were the warmth and tenderness of his family life, the satisfaction of work well done, the knowledge that the joys of music would grow more intense. And, on the other, the suffering of the world.

Jacques Feschotte

Young Albert Schweitzer was a sensitive child. It troubled him that most of his school companions were poorer than he was. He would not wear an overcoat in winter because the others did not have that luxury. He always sided with the bullied or weak pupils. These were early signs of an extraordinary compassion for the sick that was to take over his adult life.

Albert was the son of a clergyman, Louis, who became pastor of the church in Grunsbach, a village in the Munster valley, Alsace. Albert had a happy family life, and he loved the freedom he felt in the hills around his home. His concern even extended to the animal life he found there. Every night the boy prayed that God would keep the animals safe.

Albert had everything: he adored his parents, he was a clever student, and he loved books. Pastor Louis taught his young son to love music and the Bible. Both became his passion. When his singing teacher played on the piano with one finger, Albert asked her why she wasn't playing 'properly', with harmony. Enthusiastically he played the hymn with his own four-part harmony. He was deeply ashamed when he realised that she could not play like him. He was very talented and became a famous musician.

Albert was fascinated with religion, especially the Bible. It inspired him and at the same time invited his analytical mind to question some of the stories. How, for example, could Jesus grow up in poverty if the wise men had brought gold as a gift! Later he was criticised for his interpretations, but he was a natural biblical scholar.

On leaving school Albert could not decide between music and religion as a career. So he opted for a gap year in Paris to study music and then a place at Strasbourg to study Religion and Philosophy. He went on to take doctorates in both, and chose to be a pastor like his father.

By the age of 25 Albert was already an energetic, well-known musician, university professor, writer of philosophical works and pastor. But he was restless and felt drawn to follow Jesus, the Man of Suffering, more closely. It was not enough to teach about Jesus; he had to act like Jesus.

Albert made the decision to leave his brilliant career behind him at the age of 30. He resigned, retrained as a doctor and announced he was going to **Lambarene**, in Africa, to help the sick and dying. In 1912 he married Helene Bresslau, who trained as a nurse to help him. Their work in Africa was delayed when war broke out in 1914 and they were deported as prisoners of war. But he returned when war was over, and made Lambarene famous throughout the world. He died at his hospital in 1965.

The hospital at Lambarene

In 1913 Albert and Helene Schweitzer left Europe to set up a hospital at Lambarene, a deserted mission station on the crocodile-infested Ogowe River, in the heart of French Equatorial Africa (now Gabon). The patients, living in deep jungle, suffered from snake bites, malaria, ulcers and pneumonia, but the worst diseases were leprosy and sleeping sickness.

Albert took the advice of one of the first patients, Joseph, and set up simple buildings, refusing to 'import' European styles that would bewilder the Africans. (Joseph remained Albert's assistant for fifty years). The work developed, but in 1917 the German couple were interned in France, a two-year imprisonment which ruined their health. Helene never fully recovered from dysentery and TB. Albert had to return to Africa without her and their new daughter. He returned periodically to France to be with them and to raise money by giving music recitals.

The hospital became famous, especially as Albert continued to write important papers and books. He wrote passionately against slavery and religious prejudice. In 1953 he received the Nobel Peace Prize for his selfless work. With the prize money he built a new leper hospital. He received much criticism over the years – from the Church for his unorthodox biblical views, from the colonialists for daring to criticise their exploitation of the African people, and later for his stand against nuclear armament. The brilliant German doctor, philosopher, pastor and musician died in 1965, having heroically embodied the ethical principle which he called 'Reverence for Life'.

Father Damien of Molokai

Leprosy is a terrible disease which today can be easily treated. This was not always so. Lepers had to be taken from their families and never allowed to return. Leper colonies were lonely places.

When Father Damien, a Belgian priest, volunteered to go out to the South Seas as a missionary in 1863, he was so shocked by the cruelty of this disease that he offered to live on **Molokai** leper colony. He became doctor, nurse, builder, priest and friend. He was loved because he gave back to the sufferers a sense of their dignity. Damien caught leprosy himself and died with his people. His death in 1889 was more important than his life because news of his heroism spread worldwide, and stirred the world to find a cure for the disease.

What the Scriptures say:

The greatest love a person can have for his friends is to give his life for them. John 15:13

Summary

1875 Albert Schweitzer born

1893 Studied music in Paris

1895 University in Strasbourg

1895 Degree in theology

1899 Doctorate in Philosophy

1900 Doctorate in Theology
Taught at the university
Pastor in local church

1919 Daughter born. For next 45 years in Africa or fund-raising in Europe

1953 Nobel Peace Prize

1965 Died

Quick questions

1. Describe the life of Albert Schweitzer.
2. Do you think it was a remarkable life? Say why.
3. In what way was Dr Schweitzer a controversial figure?
4. Who was Father Damien?

MOLOKAI
BRUSSELS
HAWAII
DAMIEN
OF MOLOKAI
B· 1840 · D· 1889

CALCUTTA
MOTHER TERESA
B•1910•D•1997

MOTHER TERESA

Let us do something beautiful for God.

The worst disease of all is to be unwanted, uncared for and unloved.

There are poor people everywhere, but the real poverty is that no one wants them.

Few people living today will forget one week in the summer of 1997. At the beginning of that week Diana, Princess of Wales, died in Paris; a few days later Mother Teresa died in Calcutta. The lives of these two women were totally different, yet one thing united them – their extraordinary sensitivity to the most vulnerable and lonely of outcasts.

Agnes Bojaschiu was born in 1910 in Skopje, where her Albanian parents were grocers. A thoughtful girl, she was impressed by letters written to her parish from Jesuit priests in Calcutta. Determined to follow their example, she left Yugoslavia for Dublin to train as a Loreto missionary nun. She was only 17. In 1931, now called Sister Teresa, she took her religious vows and began a teaching career in India. For twenty years she taught geography at St Mary's High School, Calcutta, a smart oasis in a city of appalling squalor.

Sister Teresa always encouraged her middle-class pupils to help the poor. But by 1946 she felt called to do something more – to leave her comfortable convent to live in poverty, alongside the beggars and the dying. With papal permission she left the Loreto nuns in 1948 and, after basic medical training, took a room in the slums. She was joined by some former pupils and, in 1950, she and twelve young novices became the first sisters of a new congregation, the **Missionaries of Charity.**

Two years later the city authorities gave Mother Teresa a disused building where she took the dying destitutes from off the streets. (This hospice was later filmed by the English journalist, Malcolm Muggeridge; this film introduced Mother Teresa to a world-wide audience.) The congregation grew very quickly with hundreds of educated young women courageously embracing strict poverty and discipline. Mother Teresa had bought her white and blue sari for just 4 rupees (£5.60 today).

The sisters only possess two sets of clothes, a pair of sandals and a crucifix. They sleep in dormitories, eat simply and travel by foot. They spend several hours in prayer and for the rest of the day attend to the sick, comfort the dying, rescue abandoned babies, teach orphans, nurse lepers or visit poor families.

In 1963 Mother Teresa founded the Missionary Brothers of Charity to work in partnership with her sisters. She then founded the Sisters of the Word and the Brothers of the Word as two contemplative congregations. In 1969 her attention turned to lay people, and her **International Association of Co-Workers** was founded. Mother Teresa became a well-known figure, addressing world leaders and receiving humanitarian awards, including the Nobel Peace Prize. She was praised by the Pope, admired by Princess Diana, and loved by the poor and her thousands of Sisters, Brothers and co-workers. She described her life as *'trying to do God's will with a smile'*. When she died the world mourned.

Diana, Princess of Wales

Half a century separated the tall princess and the little nun, but the two became improbable friends. Diana is known to have admired Mother Teresa and acknowledged her as an inspiration. Both women used their high public profile to make the world aware of suffering. Unlike Mother Teresa, Diana made no claim to base her life on the Gospel; indeed many criticise her lifestyle as selfish and self-seeking. Yet Mother Teresa once said, *'I admire her a lot. She is doing God's work here on earth.'* The elderly nun was referring to Diana's public support for land-mine victims and her outgoing welcome towards AIDS sufferers.

Cardinal Basil Hume, the leader of Roman Catholics in England, celebrated a Requiem Mass for the princess. He finished his address with these words:

> *'Farewell, then, Diana.*
> *The agonies of the heart and the anguish of the mind were often your companions in life. They were your teachers, too, for from them you learned understanding, compassion and kindness. They are your finest legacy to us. Thank you for all the good you did. Thank you for the joy you gave to many. Thank you for being like the rest of us, flawed but lovable, and above all loved by God.'*

The Cardinal's words reflect the Christian belief that all human beings (including the outstanding Christians described in this book) are flawed by sin and weakness, yet capable of generous, even heroic compassion and love for others. In this they are Christ-like.

What the Scriptures say:

There was a man suffering from a dreaded skin-disease. When he saw Jesus, he threw himself down and begged him, 'Sir, if you want to, you can make me clean!' Jesus stretched out his hand and touched him. 'I do want to', he answered, 'Be clean!' At once the disease left the man.

Luke 5:12-13

Summary

1910 Agnes Bojaschiu born

1927 Went to Dublin to become a Loreto Sister

1931 As Sister Teresa, took first vows

Began teaching in India at St Mary's School, Calcutta

1948 Left Loreto nuns and took a medical course

1950 Founded Missionaries of Charity

1952 First House for the Dying

1963 Founded Missionary Brothers

1969 Association of Co-Workers founded

1979 Nobel Peace Prize

1997 Died in Calcutta

Quick questions

1. Write a short account of the life of Mother Teresa.
2. Describe the life of a Missionary of Charity.
3. Why were Mother Teresa and Princess Diana such kindred spirits?
4. In what way is the quotation from Luke (above) appropriate to represent the spirit of the princess and the nun?

DAME CICELY SAUNDERS
B 1918

DAME CICELY SAUNDERS

You need to care for the whole person, not just attend to their needs.

If you are angry, you so often find that God is beside you. He is just as angry at the situation, and he is the one who can give you the strength to get through it.

In 1980 an English doctor, Cicely Saunders, was made a Dame of the British Empire in the Honours List. This was in recognition of her pioneering work in nursing the dying. She is recognised as the founder of the **Hospice Movement**. That same year, aged 62, she married a Polish artist.

Cicely was born in Barnet, North London, in 1918. After unhappy school days and unsure of a future career, she went to Oxford to study philosophy, politics and economics. In 1939, to her parents' dismay, she left Oxford to train for nursing; the war had made her determined to work in a caring profession. Only after she qualified at St Thomas' Hospital in 1944 did she discover that her weak back made nursing impossible. She continued training and became a medical social worker. About this time Cicely became a Christian and felt a desire to serve God in her work.

The year 1947 was important for her. She fell in love with David Tasma, a dying cancer patient. His loneliness and fear touched her deeply and she resolved to devote her life to help the incurable sick. Dying patients were often abandoned by doctors. They were simply given drugs to smother the pain, but helped in no other way. Cicely went back to medical school again, and in 1957 qualified as a doctor. She worked part-time at St Luke's Hospital for the Dying in Bayswater, and did research on the control of pain at St Mary's, Paddington, and with the Catholic nuns at St Joseph's Hospice, Hackney.

After years of study and fund-raising, Dr Saunders was ready to set up her hospice. The name 'hospice' goes back to the medieval monks who received travellers as guests (*hospes* in Latin), offering them food and medical care. Cicely called her hospice after St Christopher, the legendary patron of travellers. Her Christian faith told her that death is only one stop on a journey towards God. Cicely's inspired idea was to make this one stopping place as comfortable and caring as possible.

St Christopher's Hospice

A hospice is different from a hospital, where nurses are rushed and visits limited. At St Christopher's, the sixty-two patients are cared for by ninety nurses, together with other staff and volunteer helpers. Family and friends are always welcomed and helped with their own problems of loss and fear. The hospice works in four different areas: care of the patients, home care, teaching, and further research. Cicely describes her hospice as a village, cheerful and friendly, with people of all ages living together. When she built it she had no idea that it would become the model for hospices throughout the world.

Dame Cicely's great contribution to medicine has been her discovery that pain control (**palliative care**) is possible, and can allow patients to die in dignity and without fear. Many say that if hospice nursing became universally available no one would ever think about euthanasia.

Doctor Sheila Cassidy

Sheila Cassidy is another Christian doctor whose faith inspires her work in the medical field. She became well known in 1975, when the British Government put pressure on the Pinochet regime in Chile to release Sheila from prison, where she was being tortured. Her crime was to have given medical aid to an injured revolutionary. On release, she returned to England and spoke out against the violation of human rights.

Sheila was educated in an Australian convent and at 16 felt a 'call' to commit her life to God. She eventually studied medicine in Sydney and Oxford, and worked at the Radcliffe Infirmary before going to Chile in 1971. Sheila tried her vocation in a convent, but found she needed to be alongside suffering and distressed people. (Her experience in Chile never leaves her.) Like Cicely Saunders, Sheila directed her compassion to the hospice movement, and for some years was director of St Luke's Hospice in Plymouth. Today she works with people suffering from abuse, rejection or acute loneliness. She consciously tries to walk with them in the shadow of Christ's cross.

What the Scriptures say:

Jesus cried out . . . 'Father! In your hands I place my spirit!' He said this and died. Luke 23:46

DR. SHEILA CASSIDY
B• 1937
CHILE
SANTIAGO

Healing and caring

It would be quite wrong to presume that only Christian people care about those who suffer. This is evident from the number of organisations that work to relieve pain, locally and world-wide. Perhaps you have raised money to support Save the Children Fund, Oxfam, UNICEF, Children in Need or Comic Relief (Red Nose Day). The United Nations set a standard when in 1948 it produced its 'Universal Declaration of Human Rights'. The charter stated that *'Human rights are fundamental to our nature. Without them we cannot live as human beings.'* The World Council of Churches endorsed this by stating: *'No rights are possible without the basic guarantees for life, including the right to adequate food, to guaranteed health-care and to decent housing . . .'* Every day, very ordinary people are giving their time, energy and money to try and achieve this equality. There is a very long way to go.

Summary

1918 Cicely Saunders born

1937 Went to Oxford

1939 Abandoned Oxford for a nursing career

1944 Qualified as a nurse at St Thomas' Hospital

1945 Medical social worker

1947 Met David Tasma

1957 Qualified as a doctor
Researched use of drugs

1961 St Christopher's Hospice

1980 Married Polish artist
Made a Dame (equivalent to a knighthood)
Work continues in research and care

Quick questions

1. Describe the life of Dame Cicely Saunders.
2. What is a hospice?
3. Why did Dame Cicely call her hospice after St Christopher?
4. Describe the life of Doctor Sheila Cassidy.

INTERNATIONAL COMMITTEE OF THE RED CROSS
UNICEF
NSPCC terence higgins trust WDM
since 1948
Direct Relief INTERNATIONAL
CANADIAN FEED THE CHILDREN
CAFOD
Médecins Sans Frontières
Global Volunteers
Fair Trade
FRIENDS OF THE THIRD
Shelter VSO United Nations
OXFAM
www.idealist.org
child poverty action
eurodad
TEARFUND
The Children's Society
GENEVE
CARE
CAAT
MAG
IDA
CIIR
ICFC
ITD Group
CRY
CARE AND RELIEF FOR THE YOUNG
Christian Aid
Safe Horizon
Universal Declaration of Human Rights
adopted and proclaimed by the General Assembly of the United Nations
resolution 217 A(111) of 10 December 1948
Article 1.
All human beings are born free and equal in dignity and rights.
They are endowed with reason and concience and should act towards
one another in a spirit of brotherhood.
2001

SUMMARY ON HEALING

The Gospel is about setting people free. The theme of Jesus' teaching was always freedom; not the political freedom that could have come with the overthrow of the Romans, but the freedom of those in the Kingdom of God. Jesus preached that people needed liberation from selfishness and prejudice, from ignorance and fear, from sickness of body and mind.

The many healing miracles in the Gospel are liberation stories. The evangelists, for example, clearly believed that the blind were liberated from more than bad eyesight. The Christians described in this section of the book were aware of this too. Albert Schweitzer cured thousands of patients as their doctor, but his distress at the exploitation of the African people made him work to heal colonial prejudice. St Vincent de Paul initiated health care for the poor but also worked to heal the rich of their selfishness, and comfortable clergy of their apathy.

Mother Teresa wrote: *'The biggest disease today is not leprosy or tuberculosis, but rather the feeling of being unwanted, uncared for and deserted by everybody'.* Diana, Princess of Wales, understood that very well. Cicely Saunders and Sheila Cassidy minister to the dying and help heal the fear and loneliness that can accompany the approach of death.

It is not only Christians who work to 'set people free'. This is evident from the number of people who contribute to, or work for, the hundreds of organisations set up to relieve pain, poverty and deprivation.

GLOSSARY

Association of Co-workers — An international lay organisation founded by Mother Teresa to assist her work for the poor

Daughters of Charity — Religious congregation of women founded by St Vincent de Paul and St Louise de Marillac. Today it is the largest religious community in the Catholic Church

Hospice Movement — Movement started by Cicely Saunders to treat the dying in places where individual needs can be met and the whole family cared for

Lambarene — African hospital founded by Albert Schweitzer

Missionaries of Charity — Religious order founded by Mother Teresa of Calcutta

Molokai — Leper colony where Father Damien lived and died

Palliative care — Pain control to allow patients to die with dignity

SVP Society — Lay organisation founded by students in 1830, in Paris. From Catholic parishes members care for the local sick and needy

Vincentians — Religious congregation of men founded by St Vincent de Paul in seventeenth-century France

QUESTIONS

1. Look through Luke's Gospel and make a record of incidents where Jesus showed compassion for the sick and outcast.
2. Describe the life and work of one Christian who has dedicated his/her life to relieve suffering.
3. 'I don't believe in a God who allows so much suffering in the world.'
   How would you respond to such a statement? Show different points of view in your answer.

SECTION 5: EQUALITY

Do for others just what you want them to do for you.

Luke 6:31

Introduction

This section describes some of those people whose faith has inspired them to fight to improve the lives of those on the margins of society.

Christians have usually been in the forefront of movements working to promote equality for all people. But it has to be said that the Churches have sometimes failed to treat all people as equals, even though the Christian ideal is firmly based on the belief that everyone is created by God and loved by him equally.

Jesus set the example by his actions and teaching. He showed unusual openness to Roman officers, Samaritans, tax collectors, women and all the other groups discriminated against by his contemporary Jewish society. The first Christians learnt quickly; Paul was soon preaching to the Greeks in Athens: *'From one man he (God) created all races of mankind and made them live throughout the whole earth'* Acts 17:26. He told the Colossians: *'There is no longer any distinction between Gentiles and Jews, between slaves and free men . . . but Christ is in all'* (Colossians 3:11).

WILLIAM WILBERFORCE

They call me a fanatic. If to be feelingly alive to the sufferings of others is to be a fanatic, I am one of the most incurable fanatics ever permitted to be at large.

From a speech to the House of Commons, June 1816

Jesus' admonition, *'Do for others just what you want them to do for you'* seems common sense. But the world has never learnt this lesson very well. One of the greatest abuses of human rights was the slave trade, which dominated the sixteenth to eighteenth centuries, following the European conquest of South and Central America. Millions of Africans were sold to work on plantations in North and South America. These slaves had no personal rights and were treated as property. Slave owners would not want that for themselves!

In 1788 an English politician, William Wilberforce, began a nineteen-year struggle to abolish this slave trade. William was born in Hull in 1759, the son of a wealthy merchant. An intelligent boy, he went to Cambridge University before being elected a Member of Parliament for Hull when only 21 years old. He was elected to the larger constituency of Yorkshire four years later. In the same year he took a European tour and whilst travelling was converted to Christianity. This greatly influenced his political life.

He is best known for his concern over slavery. Supported by Thomas Clarkson and the Quakers, he succeeded in 1807 in getting abolition of the slave trade through Parliament. He then worked to extend this abolition abroad and to secure the total abolition of all types of slavery. But his poor health meant retirement from Westminster in 1825, eight years before his ambition was finally achieved in 1833, the year of his death.

William was an active evangelical Christian, a member of the 'Clapham Sect' who worked to improve community life. He wrote *A Practical View of Christianity* whilst campaigning for slaves.

Jesus, Jews and slavery

The rich have always asked others to work on their behalf, and that will probably never change. Career-minded women today pay for nannies to bring up their children; wealthy or royal households employ butlers, chefs, housekeepers and gardeners. Serving one another is the way our society works. It only becomes unjust when one group considers itself superior to the other and abuses human rights.

Jesus had respect for servants because he was a Jew. The Book of Deuteronomy (part of Jewish Law) required masters to treat their slaves with dignity and generosity. A slave had to be given his freedom after six years, and was never sent away empty-handed, but given livestock, corn and wine (see Deuteronomy 15:12-18).

Children and slavery

It was not until 1926 that slavery was internationally condemned. The **League of Nations** called for its total suppression. In 1948 this view was reaffirmed by the **United Nations** in the **Universal Declaration of Human Rights**. In 1956 fifty-one nations met in Geneva to condemn newer forms of servitude, especially those relating to women and children. Some children, for example, were being adopted just to act as servants. Abuse of children is nothing new.

Lord Shaftesbury (7th Earl) entered Parliament in 1826 and became the champion for poor children. He brought about laws prohibiting employment of women and children in coal mines (1842); he cut factory working hours and established 'ragged schools' for neglected children, to take them out of child labour markets.

Unhappily his ideals are still not respected universally. Today 55 million children are still being exploited. In the poor 'South', children as young as 6 are left to survive as **street children**, surviving by cleaning car windows or selling matches. Children in India are employed long hours, in appalling conditions, sewing footballs or making trainers for the rich 'North'. The **United Nations Declaration on the Rights of the Child** is ignored by employers and it is left to conscientious individuals and organisations like **UNICEF**, Christian Aid and CAFOD to fight for the rights of children (see page 89).

What the Scriptures say:

Do not cheat a poor and needy hired servant, whether he is a fellow-Israelite or a foreigner living in one of your towns. Each day . . . pay him . . . he needs the money. Do not deprive foreigners and orphans of their rights . . . Remember you were slaves in Egypt and that the Lord your God set you free.

Deuteronomy 24:14-15, 17-18

Summary

1759 Wilberforce born

1776 To Cambridge

1780 MP for Hull

1784 MP for Yorkshire and converted to Christianity

1788 Campaign for abolition of slavery began

1807 Bill through Parliament

1825 Ill health, retired

1833 Died. Abolition of slavery across Empire

1926 League of Nations called for total ban on slavery

1956 UN condemn new forms of slavery

Quick questions

1. Jesus preached equality by word and actions. Give examples.
2. Show how Jesus learnt respect for slaves from his Jewish Scriptures.
3. Write a paragraph on William Wilberforce and slavery.
4. Who was Lord Shaftesbury?

WILLIAM WILBERFORCE
B • 1759 • D • 1833

LORD SHAFTESBURY
B 1801 D 1885

TREVOR HUDDLESTON

> ***Trevor Huddleston was a sentinel of freedom and brotherhood, a crusader against racism, a man of conviction and compassion and a champion of universal justice and peace.*** **Sonia Gandhi**

The abolition of the slave trade may have given black Africans some relief, but discrimination and prejudice against them lived on, reaching a frightening intensity under the **apartheid** system in South Africa. Apartheid is the name given by the white government to the policy of 'separate development'. It gave the white minority all the privileges and discriminated against the black population, who were given poor land, poor education, no rights and no vote.

In 1943 a young Anglican missionary priest left Liverpool for South Africa. His name was Trevor Huddleston. He was to become the man responsible for opening the eyes of the world to the evils of this political system in South Africa. Trevor was born in 1913, the only son of Sir Ernest Huddleston. He was educated at Lancing College and Christ Church, Oxford, before going to Wells Theological College. He was ordained priest in 1937. Fr Huddleston joined the Anglican Community of the Resurrection in 1941 and two years later was sent by the community as priest-in-charge of Sophiatown, in the diocese of Johannesburg.

The young priest quickly became known as the 'champion of universal justice and peace' because he could not remain silent when, from 1950 onwards, he saw the policy of racial segregation deprive his many parishioners of their human rights. Huddleston found Sophiatown a wonderful place, where the mixed community of 60,000 people – Africans, Indians, Chinese and Pakistanis – lived in utter poverty, patience and joyful exuberance. The people loved him and he worked tirelessly to give them a sense of dignity. When Sophiatown was threatened with bulldozers he spoke out fearlessly against the government officials. But after thirteen years Fr Huddleston was called back to England where his religious community were getting anxious about this outspokenness. He seemed to be too political in their eyes.

On his return Huddleston wrote about the whole situation in *Naught For Your Comfort*, and he never stopped campaigning for the repeal of the apartheid law. Overnight he became the most well-known and highly respected English priest. He was made a bishop and later worked in Tanzania and Mauritius. For some years he lived in the East End of London, quietly setting up schemes to keep children off the streets and to provide for disabled children. He was like a magnet to young people who recognised a good man who understood their aspirations. A former Dean of St Paul's Cathedral wrote of him:

> *'The charisma and authority of this determined, laughing, radical bishop has been felt wherever he has worked . . . He lived out the essentials – prayer and righteous action. The strength of the Church of England lay not in the traditional establishment but in its complete inability to control the spiritual power of Huddleston. He captivated younger Christians as did no other religious leader in the second half of the twentieth century.'*

Archbishop Huddleston lived long enough to see the apartheid system broken and Nelson Mandela elected president of South Africa. He died at Mirfield amongst his religious community in 1998.

What the Scriptures say:

> *Love is patient and kind; it is not jealous or conceited or proud . . . love is not happy with evil, but is happy with the truth. Love never gives up, and its faith, hope and patience never fail.*
> 1 Corinthians 13:4, 6-7

What the bishops say:

> *For a Christian, racial prejudice is an intolerable evil and has to be fought at every level where it shows itself, because man is made in the image of God . . . because any offence against the dignity of man is not an offence against man alone, but a blasphemy, a denial of God's truth.*
> Bishop Trevor Huddleston

> *When God encounters injustice, oppression, or exploitation, he takes sides. Then God and the Bible are subversive of such a situation.*
> Bishop Helder Camara

Politics and religion

It could be said that Jesus came not to comfort the afflicted but to afflict the comfortable. Trevor Huddleston was a good disciple – he had the courage to challenge politicians, Church authority and 'comfortable' Christians. A company chairman commented: *'For me he is a dangerous man.*

He makes me do good things I do not want to do, and stops me doing the bad things I had intended.'

Christians are sometimes accused of 'meddling' in politics. Indeed, some Christians would argue that Jesus' message was entirely spiritual. Bishop Huddleston was accused of mis-using his position when he challenged the political system of South Africa and worked alongside founder-members of the **African National Congress**. With Oliver Tambo, a teacher in his school, and Walter Sisulu (who was later in prison for twenty-seven years alongside Nelson Mandela) Trevor Huddleston led protests, organised strikes and made hundreds of public speeches against the regime.

Many Christians today agree with Bishop Huddleston that the Gospels show how Jesus challenged authority when it abused its power. Jesus refused to take up arms but he used words to argue for the rights of ordinary people. In this way he was political. Huddleston often shocked traditional Church of England members with his outspoken words: he recommended dialogue with other world religions; he urged the Church to welcome women into full ministry. If these ideas disturbed Church leaders, his words and actions had the opposite effect on world organisations. He received many international awards and in 1997 was made a Knight Commander in the Honours list for his outstanding part in healing British-South African relations.

Summary

1913 Huddleston born

1937 Ordained

1941 Joined Community of the Resurrection

1943 To Sophiatown in South Africa

1956 Recalled to England

1960 Made Bishop of Masasi

1968 Bishop of Stepney

1978 Bishop of Mauritius

1981-94 President of Anti-Apartheid Movement

1983-98 President of National Peace Council

1998 Died

Quick questions

1. What are prejudice and discrimination? Give examples.
2. Write 100 words describing the life and work of Trevor Huddleston.
3. In what ways should a disciple of Jesus 'afflict the comfortable'?
4. Is it possible to be a disciple of Jesus and not be political?
5. What was 'apartheid'?

TREVOR HUDDLESTON B•1913 • D•1998•
WE DEMAND SA IMPLEMENT RESOLUTION
WELCOME TO OUR POLICE STATE

MARTIN
LUTHER
KING
B. 1929.
D. 1968.
1963
1964
MEMPHIS
ATLANTA
BIRMINGHAM
MONTGOMERY

MARTIN LUTHER KING

I have a dream that my four little children will one day live in a nation where they will not be judged by the colour of their skin but by the content of their character. I have a dream today!

In 1968 a white man, James Earl Ray, assassinated the Baptist minister, Martin Luther King, in Memphis, Tennessee. The single gunshot seemed to reverberate across a shocked world. Martin Luther King has become the prophet and martyr for the cause of equal rights and respect for the black population of the world.

Martin was born in Atlanta, Georgia, in 1929. He was the son of the Reverend and Mrs Martin Luther King, Senior. Living in the heart of the American South, the family knew the injustices heaped upon the descendants of the four million African slaves shipped to America centuries before. Although slavery had been ended by Abraham Lincoln in 1865, black Americans still lived in dreadful conditions. A policy of segregation (as in South Africa) existed. Black Americans were not allowed to use the same transport, restaurants or bars as white Americans. They attended separate schools. The **Ku Klux Klan** organisation even advocated a return to slavery.

Martin Luther King Junior studied to be a Baptist minister, like his father, and in 1954 began his ministry in Montgomery, Alabama. He had been married the year before to Coretta Scott. At this time the **Black Power Movement**, led by Malcolm X, believed that violence was the only way to bring about equality. The young church minister disagreed, and in 1955 he began to work actively for equal rights insisting on a *policy of non-violence*. When a black woman, Rosa Parks, refused to give up her bus seat to a white man she was arrested. Martin Luther King organised a 'bus-boycott' – and the black community refused to use buses until segregation was removed. The activities developed into the **Civil Rights Movement**, and by 1960 Luther King was its leader. Gradually changes were made following the endless campaigning. He led peaceful marches and sit-ins which were often broken up violently by the police. In 1965 a march to Montgomery was broken up with tear gas and clubs. It was seen on television. The brutality shocked people and a few months later the Voting Rights Act was passed.

Life for the Luther King family was uncomfortable and frightening because this peace-loving man was confronted with violence: his family received death threats; his house was bombed; he was stabbed, stoned and imprisoned. Yet he never wavered from preaching forgiveness, tolerance and love. Not all white people opposed him and in 1964 he received the Nobel Peace Prize. Martin Luther King Junior was only 39 when he died. In his last sermon he had said:

> *'If any of you are around when I have to meet my day, I don't want a long funeral. I'd like somebody to mention that day that Martin Luther King tried to give his life serving others, and I want you to say I tried to love and serve humanity.'*

What the Scriptures say:

> *For even the Son of Man did not come to be served; he came to serve and to give his life to redeem many people.* Mark 10:45
>
> *Take up your cross and follow me.*
> Mark 8:34, adapted

Words of Martin Luther King:

> *The way of non-violence means a willingness to suffer and sacrifice. It may mean going to jail. If such is the case the resister must be willing to fill the jail houses of the South. It may even mean physical death. But if physical death is the price that a man must pay to free his children and his white brethren from a permanent death of spirit, then nothing could be more redemptive.*
> *Stride Towards Freedom*, published 1958

What the Churches say:

> *Sometimes it is not adequate simply to care for those damaged by life and by society. Sometimes the social structures that are causing the damage need to be challenged.*
> *Celebrating the Anglican Way*, page 149

Women who fought for freedom

Martin Luther King was not the first black American to fight peacefully for human rights and equality for his people. Amongst others, two women had prepared the way.

Sojourner Truth, who was born in 1797, was a slave. She won her freedom and chose to spend the rest of her life campaigning for equal rights for black people. She became a wandering Christian preacher. Before Emily Pankhurst had begun her fight for women's right to vote in

Britain, Sojourner had campaigned for this in the American South. She died in 1883.

Harriet Tubman was born in Maryland, in the American South, in 1821. She too was born a slave, but in 1849 she escaped and avoided capture. She spent much of her life helping other runaway slaves to escape to the freer North. Harriet helped to run the Underground Railroad, which was a series of hiding places in barns and cellars. The escaping slaves hid in these 'safe' places and received food and clothing as they fled north. Slave owners offered 40,000 dollars for her capture. She worked for the northern armies in the Civil War and, when the war ended and slavery was abolished, she devoted the rest of her life to raising money for black schools. She died in 1913, aged 92. Only sixteen years later Martin Luther King was born.

Summary

1929 Luther King born in Atlanta

1953 Married Coretta Scott

1954 Baptist minister in Montgomery, Alabama

1955 Civil Rights work began

1964 Nobel Peace Prize

1965 Voting Rights Act passed

1968 Assassinated in Memphis

Quick questions

1. Why was the American South the scene of racial injustice?
2. Write a description of Martin Luther King's life.
3. Describe two women who left slavery and worked for justice.

Longer questions

- In what way was Martin Luther King's campaign a non-violent one?
- Why do you think he believed in non-violence?
- Were the 'Black Power' people being more realistic to presume violence was necessary to achieve the same ends?

SOJOURNER
TRUTH
B• 1797
D• 1883
HARRIET
TUBMAN
B• 1821
D• 1913

LIBERIA
SOMALIA
SEAN
DEVEREUX
B 1965 D 1993

SEAN DEVEREUX

While my heart beats I have to do what I think I can do – that is to help those who are less fortunate than ourselves.
Sean Devereux

He was our hero. **Dermot Devereux**

About twenty-five years after Martin Luther King's death another young man was shot for working peacefully for the human rights of disadvantaged people. He was Sean Devereux, an energetic, smiling PE teacher from England, who was working as a United Nations volunteer in Somalia.

Sean and his sisters, Tanya and Theresa, were brought up in a loving, secure and comfortable Irish Catholic home. He attended the Salesian College in Farnborough, and later trained for teaching at Loughborough University. His father worked for an airline company so the family enjoyed wonderful holidays abroad. Sean especially loved Africa. From the age of 14 Sean, a good athlete, knew exactly what he wanted to do. He had learnt from parents and teachers to put other people first and to seek justice for the underprivileged. He was always a fun-loving and popular student in school and was appointed school captain. A teacher said he had *'qualities of ready friendship, firm leadership and organising ability'.* His first teaching post was at the Salesian College, Chertsey, but after a short while he joined the staff of St Francis Salesian School in Tappita, Liberia.

Sean sent his family charming videos of the daily routine, where the happy children affectionately called him 'Mr Sean'. A former teacher of his, Fr Brian, also went to Tappita and was astonished at the 'amazing relationship' he quickly built up with 900 lively children. *'He won everybody over with his cheerfulness and transparent dedication, seeming to belong to all.'* But Sean's carefree happiness in Liberia came to a sudden end in 1990 when civil war devastated the land, bringing massacre and famine. He was out of town organising a sports event when the rebel troops attacked and he never returned to Tappita. He had the anguish of seeing some of his boys commandeered into the army as child soldiers. He joined the United Nations as a volunteer relief worker and with enormous courage worked in the front line. Sean was fearless when he observed the corruption amongst the authorities and the exploitation of the young boys. He even confronted a psychopathic rebel leader in an effort to free a former pupil of his from the army. He worked with the Salesian Fathers to rehabilitate many traumatised child soldiers after their release.

Time and again Sean Devereux fell foul of the military leaders in the conflict and suffered beatings and imprisonment. On one occasion his life was saved when a former Fourth Grade student recognised Sean being beaten up by a drunken soldier. Sean angered the authorities because he refused to lie; he refused to compromise and turn a blind eye to corruption; and he distributed food on the basis of need, not on the basis of tribal identity. Finally Sean was restricted to Monrovia, away from the front line, so he volunteered to leave Liberia for the more dangerous mission in Somalia. He joined UNICEF and became responsible for the huge relief operation in Kismayo.

Once again Sean was expected by the authorities to compromise his sense of justice. He spoke out bravely and perhaps naïvely against corruption. His greatest horror was the realisation that the arms given to his young pupils came from the 'civilised world', Britain, France and the USA. Sean's work in war-torn Somalia was highly praised by UNICEF. Journalists were quick to interview such an honest, idealistic young man, and with typical bravery Sean criticised the evils of the war. His honesty probably cost him his life. He was shot in the head by an unknown as he was returning to quarters one evening in January 1993. All who knew him felt it had been the greatest honour and privilege to have been his friend.

Voluntary Work Overseas

Many young people share Sean Devereux's concern for disadvantaged and exploited children. Sean found a way, through the Salesian Missions and the United Nations, to put his ideals into action. Every year hundreds of young men and women offer to take part in schemes set up to bring the rich North and the poor South together. One scheme is run by the De La Salle Brothers, who send young volunteers during their summer holidays to work on school and mission building sites in Asia, Africa or the Caribbean. **Stephanie Pinnington** went to Southern India on this scheme.

Stephanie in Boys' Village, Tamil Nadu

'Four flights later and we finally arrived at our destination – Boys' Village. It was the middle of the night. I was so tired but I do remember vividly the shadows

of sleeping boys round the edge of the yard. It was too hot in their rooms. Two De La Salle brothers showed us to our quarters – the art room. The boys had cleaned it out and moved in twelve wooden beds. We felt embarrassed because the children only slept on mats on the floor. The art room was our home for the next five weeks.

'I woke early and looked out of the window at coconut plantations and mountains in the distance. When I went out into the warm air I saw "welcome" chalked out on the ground outside our room. It faded over the weeks although the children's actual welcome never faded!

'Boys' Village is an orphanage run by the De La Salle brothers in Southern India. The boys, aged between 7 and 15, come from poor, even destitute, backgrounds. Some had been abandoned. But they are the lucky ones because they have the opportunity for a better future. At the Village they are given a home, an education and, most important of all, much care and love.

'We were there to work alongside local people to help make structural improvements to Boys' Village. They needed more accommodation for visitors. We also helped to build new paths, we dug drainage trenches, and even did some re-roofing!

'Each day the boys would get up very early, about 5 am. They did some schoolwork and then had a simple breakfast of rice. Then they caught the school bus. They were so keen to learn that when they returned from school in the evening some of our group gave them English lessons. But they were not the only ones to learn.

'Through our daily interaction with the children, the brothers and the local people we gained so much. We learnt to live as a community and we learnt about ourselves – about our values and our priorities. India is an amazing, colourful country. I will never forget the warmth of the people and their courage in hardship. The boys in the Village shared their happiness and hope with us. They are an inspiration.'

Quick questions

1. Write an account of Sean Devereux's life. In what way was his life inspired by the Gospel?
2. Sean and Stephanie went out to help the children. Who do you think gained most, the children or Sean and Stephanie? Explain your answer.

STEPHANIE
PINNINGTON
B•1978
AN QUIL EST LE BON DIEU

SUMMARY ON EQUALITY

It is very difficult for members of one group to accept rival groups as equals. Would it ever occur to a Tottenham Hotspur supporter to applaud the Arsenal team when they win the local derby? Prejudice is lodged deep in everyone's life. All too often we confirm our attachment to sports teams, family, country or religion by doing down rival groups.

Christian disciples of Jesus should behave differently. He taught by word and example that all people are equal as children of God. When he welcomed tax collectors, women, Samaritans and Roman officers he raised eyebrows. Unfortunately Christianity has not always learnt from Jesus. From anti-Semitism in the early Church to ethnic cleansing in Kosovo, the Christian Church has failed.

But individuals have been inspired by Jesus. Section 5 describes a few of them.

GLOSSARY

African National Congress Multi-racial nationalist organisation formed in 1912 to get the vote for all the people of South Africa

Apartheid Former White South African policy of 'separate development' which discriminated against Blacks

Black Power Movement Movement towards Black separatism in USA, in the 1960s

Civil Rights Movement Martin Luther King's policy of non-violence in the 1960s – to bring about equality

Ku Klux Klan White American secret organisation, racist and violent

League of Nations International organisation formed after World War I to solve disputes by arbitration

Street children Children from poor families (some abandoned or abused) who live on city streets in the poor South

UNICEF United Nations International Children's Fund. A voluntary organisation founded in 1946 to provide long-term health care and education for all children

United Nations Replaced League of Nations in 1945. Works for peace and security from its New York headquarters

Universal Declaration of Human Rights 1948 charter of civil and political rights drawn up by the UN. It is not legally binding

QUESTIONS

1. (a) What is prejudice?

   (b) Describe two *actual* examples of racial prejudice.

2. Write an account of the life of Trevor Huddleston.

   Show how he worked against the apartheid system. How was this work influenced by his Christianity?

3. Show how Jesus broke through the prejudices of his world. Was he ever political in his actions or words? (If so, give examples.)

   Should Church leaders be political?

SECTION 6: JUSTICE

Love the Lord your God with all your heart . . .
Love your neighbour as you love yourself.

Mark 12:30-31

Introduction

This section looks at some of the people and organisations which work to help the poorest in our world, and to bring about a change in attitude in the richer nations.

On 10 December 1948, the General Assembly of the United Nations adopted and proclaimed the Universal Declaration of Human Rights. The historic act recognised the absolute equality of all persons, and the responsibility of people to allow others to have the same rights as they would expect for themselves. This is justice. The Assembly asked all member countries to 'cause the Declaration to be disseminated, displayed, read and expounded principally in schools'.

More than fifty years later it is clear that the Declaration of Human Rights has not been adopted everywhere. Injustices exist at every level of society. In some countries the rights of the majority of the population are totally ignored. In recent years the Churches have sided with these majorities to challenge injustice and misuse of power. The Christian challenge is based on the example of Jesus.

Jesus, inspired by the Book of Deuteronomy, expresses justice as the call to love God and neighbour.

JULIAN FILOCHOWSKI

CAFOD is an expression of solidarity, of love, of our yearning for justice for the poor in the developing world.

Cardinal Basil Hume

In 1962 the Catholic bishops of England and Wales set up an agency to address the issues of injustice and unequal distribution of wealth. Since 1982 Julian Filochowski has been the Director of this agency which is called the Catholic Fund for Overseas Development – **CAFOD**.

Julian was born in Yorkshire and went to school at St Michael's College in Leeds. He graduated from Churchill College, Cambridge, with an MA in Economics, specialising in Development Economics and Statistics. Like Sean Devereux, Julian felt he wanted to share his gifts with the underprivileged, so he worked as a volunteer in Central America from 1969 to 1973. He was in Belize and Honduras, and later in Guatemala as co-ordinator of the British volunteer programme.

Julian returned to the United Kingdom in 1973 to share his practical knowledge of the developing world with the **CIIR**, the Catholic Institute for International Relations. He specialised in Latin American affairs. The CIIR is a very strong pressure group within the Catholic Church for international justice, supporting practical action with serious research into political/economic world situations.

Julian left the CIIR to work for CAFOD in 1982. Since that time he has witnessed the growth of CAFOD's work and travelled throughout Latin America, Africa and Asia. He is such a respected authority on world development that he is now a member of numerous committees and councils concerned with international justice and peace.

The work of CAFOD

'CAFOD aims to help people help themselves, involving the local community to the greatest extent possible. Projects are concerned with the causes, as well as the conditions of hunger,

disease, ignorance and poverty. CAFOD's goal is: to promote human development and social justice in witness to Christian faith and gospel values.'
CAFOD statement

The organisation now supports over 1000 projects in 75 countries. Much of the money, over £20 million per year, is raised by the annual **family fast day**. Envelopes are distributed to parishes and schools and people are encouraged to go without food and contribute the cost saved to the fund.

One of the main tasks of CAFOD is education. Many colourful books, pamphlets, posters and videos are offered to study groups and schools so that the rich North is aware of the injustices suffered by the poor South. CAFOD is not afraid to point out the weaknesses of past and present secular and religious regimes. During the 1992 Columbus celebrations they produced a video which revealed the terrible abuse of the Indian people by the Catholic Church. CAFOD worked alongside other organisations like **Christian Aid** to promote **Jubilee 2000**, a movement calling for the backlog of unpayable debts owed by the world's poorest countries to be cancelled in celebration of the Millennium. Britain responded.

Led by Julian Filochowski, CAFOD is prominent in taking part in national emergency relief programmes set up in the aftermath of world disasters – earthquakes, floods, famine and war devastation. In 1986 Julian drew CAFOD to respond to the AIDS pandemic. CAFOD now specialises in AIDS programmes.

Christian Aid

The largest Christian organisation to help the world's poor is **Christian Aid.** It was set up in 1945 by Churches in the UK and Ireland to put into action their concern for the world's poorest people. It is now part of the British Council of Churches. Every May, Christian Aid holds a national fundraising campaign. The £40 million raised annually is used in projects similar to those set up by CAFOD: self-sufficiency schemes; building schools and clinics; digging wells; supporting refugees; campaigning for landmine victims; educating this country; challenging supermarkets over unfair trading practice.

Tear Fund

Tear Fund (The Evangelical Alliance Relief Fund) is another Christian organisation that works to relieve suffering in the Developing World. Cliff Richard, the pop star, is closely associated with Tear Fund and has raised hundreds of thousands of pounds, and visited projects in action. Tear Fund's long-term projects enable people to become self-sufficient, giving the poor a sense of dignity. This is inspired by the Christian belief that every person is special and loved by God.

What the Scriptures say:

This is what Yahweh asks of you – only this, that you act justly, that you love tenderly, that you walk humbly with your God.
Micah 6:8, author's own translation

Let justice flow like a stream, and righteousness like a river that never runs dry. Amos 5:24

One of them . . . predicted that a severe famine was about to come over all the earth . . . The disciples decided that each of them would send as much as he could to help their fellow believers in Judaea. Acts 11:28-29

Christian Aid's prayer of commitment

O God, you promise a world
where those who now weep shall laugh,
those who are hungry shall feast,
those who are poor now, and excluded,
shall have your kingdom for their own.
I want this world too.
I renounce despair.
I will act for change.
I choose to be included
in your great feast of life.

Quick questions

1. Write 100 words about Julian Filochowski.
2. What is the Universal Declaration of Human Rights?
3. Describe the work of CAFOD, Tear Fund or Christian Aid.

JULIAN
FILOCHOWSKI
B. 1947
CAFOD

ITA FORD
B. 1940 . D. 1980
HONDURAS
EL SALVADOR
NICARAGUA

SISTER ITA FORD

I have come to realise that my sister was a giant. She understood before most of us understood what was happening in El Salvador. My sister was not a political agent of anyone. If anything she was an agent of Jesus Christ. **Brother of Sister Ita Ford**

Many Christians campaign for justice from their own homes, or raise money to support projects in developing countries. Others choose to go and share the poverty and pain of the most destitute. Sister Ita Ford, an American Maryknoll sister, did just that.

The Maryknoll missionary congregation was founded in 1911 in New York. Today the mother house, 'The Knoll' by the Hudson River, is a busy meeting place for missionaries. Sheila Cassidy (see page 68) describes it:

'My clearest memory of "The Knoll" is the dining room, an enormous cafeteria where over fifty women sit quietly talking at small tables, dressed in anything from Bermuda shorts to the full religious habit. . . . If you sit around for a while you'll find yourself being introduced to people: "This is Peg; she got back from Chile yesterday", or "This is Mary; she's just home from Korea". And you find that these very ordinary-looking women spent yesterday on a plane and the day before working alongside refugees or mothers whose babies are dying of malnutrition. . . . You may suddenly miss a familiar face and someone says, "Oh Bernie – she left this morning at six". And you discover that Bernie has gone back to Central America.'

Sheila Cassidy visited The Knoll after she had become friends with two Maryknoll sisters, Carla and Ita, in Chile. In 1980 Archbishop Oscar Romero (see page 129) asked for help in El Salvador, where his people were being persecuted and kept in poverty. Outspoken Christians were being killed to silence their calls for justice. In one parish alone all forty-two catechists had been murdered. Carla and Ita volunteered to take on the dangerous task of working for the poor in Salvador, under the guidance of the heroic Archbishop. Carla arrived in San Salvador just two hours after he had been shot whilst celebrating Mass. She wrote to Maryknoll that sadness, shock and fear had spread across the country. Sister Ita arrived a week later.

The two friends struggled to find what work they should do; even priests had left in despair. They wrote:

'We are pastoral workers used to having pe visit and meet. Now we have no home of our o no people – we cannot visit because of the times and the very real fear of placing others in danger because of belonging to the Church – which is one of the security forces' biggest enemies. A lot of energy goes into walking down this dark road.'

Carla and Ita suffered loneliness and fear. Bravely they struggled to help refugees, 'inventing a job daily'. On 21 August 1980 Ita pleaded with an army colonel to release missing people. As a gesture he released one prisoner to their custody. Whilst driving him home the jeep was engulfed in flash floods. Carla drowned. Ita, battered and injured, was discovered three kilometres down river. It is difficult to imagine the bewilderment and isolation that this young nun must have felt over the next months. Her letters express grief and pain. Yet her courage never faltered.

The night before she died, Ita attended a Maryknoll reunion. She enjoyed the comfort of a happy farewell dinner with her missionary sisters. The next day, 2 December 1980, she was dragged from her car with three others, raped and killed by security forces on a deserted road.

Liberation Theology

Sister Ita had begun her religious life as an ordinary teaching sister. She was happy and carefree in her convent and school, where she was much loved by the children. Her close, supportive family were surprised when she gave up such a secure life for the uncertainties of work in Latin America. Ita herself found the change dramatic.

In the 1960s there arose a new type of Catholic Church in the Third World. Following a bishops' meeting in Medellin in 1968, Church leaders called for an **Option for the Poor**. A new theology was developing, now known as **Liberation Theology**. This new way of interpreting the Gospel was not exclusively Roman Catholic, but it was led by the South and Central American Catholic theologians and missionaries. It sees earthly liberation (freedom) as the first stage of the coming of God's Kingdom. It calls on the Church to take a vigorous role in fighting for justice. This newer theology saw political activity as a necessary part of the Church's mission. It was not well received by the powerful and wealthy leaders of autocratic governments, nor even by many European Church leaders, including the Pope.

…merica at the time when …as developing. In 1979 … this time in Puebla, and …nent to work for justice …ses. Writings by four lead…s, Leonardo Boff, Gustavo …egundo and Jon Sobrino, … …urch of this new thinking. Missionaries like Sister Ita, and leaders like Archbishop Romero adopted this ideal and sought human rights for their people. They followed Jesus closely by giving their lives for the sake of the Kingdom of God.

Liberation theology gives lay people the central role. The priests and nuns step back to walk alongside the whole community rather than lead it from the front. In the developing world of the 1970s **base communities** began to replace traditional churches. Local people, peasants and professionals, were encouraged by their priests to become more active in demanding human rights. They were made conscious of their dignity and worth. The new movement was deeply rooted in the Gospel. Local house meetings began with prayer and Bible study, before decisions about local unjust situations were discussed. The greatest liberation felt by the people was the realisation that Jesus was one of them. He understood their poverty because he had shared it. Until then they had associated him with a rich Church, supported by a rich government. Sister Ita had learnt very quickly what this meant in her years in Chile, under Pinochet's rule.

The Kairos Document

In 1989 a document was drawn up and signed by a wide range of Christian organisations, communities, theologians and church leaders belonging to a broad spectrum of Christian traditions. It was an expression of deep concern over the division in Christianity between the church of the poor and the right-wing Christianity that supported privilege and power.

Christians from seven countries worked to produce this strong statement on behalf of the poor. They were from El Salvador, Guatemala, Korea, Namibia, Nicaragua, Philippines and South Africa.

What the Scriptures say:

Now as the time drew near for him to be taken up to heaven, he resolutely took the road for Jerusalem. Luke 9:51, NIV

What Church leaders say:

The world that the Church must serve is the world of the poor. It is the poor who force us to understand what is really taking place . . . the persecution of the Church is a result of defending the poor. The poor are the Body of Christ today. Through them he lives on in history.

Archbishop Oscar Romero

Summary

1968 Bishops' Conference in Medellin. Option for the Poor

1979 Commitment renewed in Puebla, Mexico

1980 Death of Archbishop Romero in El Salvador

1980 Deaths of Sister Carla and Sister Ita in El Salvador

Quick questions

1. What is Liberation Theology?
2. What are 'base communities'?
3. Describe the life and death of Sister Ita Ford.
4. Should the Church be political?

Longer question

Read the quotation from Luke's Gospel above. In what way do you think it applies to the choice made by Sister Ita?

JAIME JARAMILO

I think people are valuable for what they are, not for what they have.

Every day I thank God for everything he has given me.

We teach the children to have faith and to forgive.

Not all wealthy people in Latin America ignore the plight of the poor. Jaime Jaramilo, for example, is a very influential and successful Colombian businessman. He works in the oil industry. His comfortable childhood was far removed from the life of homeless street children, but he was deeply distressed by their suffering. Over twenty years ago, when he was a student, he saw a street child killed as she ran into the road to collect litter. The incident changed his life.

Jaime risked ridicule and even danger when he began to distribute food to the children and speak up on their behalf. He married and had a son and daughter. When his own professional life as a geophysicist became more successful and his life style more comfortable, he found it necessary to increase his work for the 'disposable' children. He rescued one 11-year-old, called Rebecca, and paid her hospital bill. To his amazement he discovered that she had contracted her illness underground, in the sewers. He went searching the sewers for other children, and with his family set up a foundation, **Fundacion Niños de los Andes**, to raise the money to rehouse and care for these 'outcast' children. His wife agreed that they should give 60 per cent of their income to help the Fundacion.

Jaime said: *'God gave me all the tools to do what he wanted. If I were a poor guy, I would never be able to do what I have done. If I didn't have money, how could I set up all these things?'* A few years ago a television programme was made about Jaime's work for these children of the sewers. It had a great effect on people, but in different ways. It inspired many generous people in England to raise money for Jaime's work, and it enabled him to build children's homes to house the most damaged and vulnerable children taken off the streets. But it also angered the authorities in Bogota, since it highlighted the failures of a government which sanctioned 'clean-up squads' to kill street children. A smear campaign was started to discredit Jaime Jaramilo. The strain broke up his marriage, though Patricia, his wife, still works for the Fundacion.

In 1996 Jaime's name was cleared, and more recently the police and other officials have worked co-operatively with him. Today many doctors and dentists give their services free to these children on the streets. It is impossible to give homes to the thousands of these children (70,000 in Bogota alone) but volunteers, including Esteban, Jaime's student son, go out on patrols to distribute food and treat the children with respect as human beings. Some of the children rescued by Jaime now work in the oil industry or similar jobs; one boy is on a tennis scholarship in Florida and another in the National Youth Orchestra. In many ways, Jaime has been a pioneer amongst the rich in treating the poor as equals.

Possible reactions to injustice

People react to poverty and injustice in different ways. Even Christians, who believe that all people are equal as children of God, disagree on how to approach the injustices that exist in the world. There are four possible reactions, according to how they read the Gospel:

1. Accepting the situation

- 'It is God's will'.
- Jesus was a pacifist who did not fight evil with anything other than acceptance of suffering.
- The poor will be rewarded in heaven.

2. Acting quietly for change

- Protesting peacefully by writing letters to governments or leading seminars on education.
- Giving generously to organisations that relieve suffering.
- Standing alongside the poor, as Sister Ita did, following Jesus' example.

3. Acting politically but peacefully

- Taking leading roles in social reform, like Martin Luther King or Jaime Jaramilo.
- Speaking out publicly and critically like Oscar Romero. Jesus certainly spoke out boldly and upset the authorities in doing so.

4. Acting violently as the 'lesser of two evils'

- Working to overthrow unjust regimes even when violence has to be used. Even Jesus acted violently when he overthrew the tables of the money changers in the Temple.

Camilo Torres

When Jaime Jaramilo was a young boy he must have heard of the death of Camilo Torres, a former Catholic priest of Bogota, who had joined revolutionary forces against the government. He was killed fighting for the rights of the poor.

Camilo was born in 1930 and became a priest in his native Colombia because he wanted to serve God in showing concern for those less fortunate than himself. His neighbours were poor farmers who were treated unjustly by rich land owners. At first he tried to work peacefully to bring the poor some share of their country's wealth. He taught them their rights and spoke up against the abuse of government power. But the government responded with military force.

Father Camilo received no support from the official Catholic Church, which at this time worked in harmony with the government. So Camilo Torres gave up his priesthood and joined up with a revolutionary group. In 1966 he was shot whilst fighting the government forces.

What the Scriptures say:

Mary said: My soul magnifies the Lord
and my spirit rejoices in God my Saviour . . .
He has put down the mighty from their seat,
and he has exalted the humble.
He has filled the hungry with good things;
and the rich he has sent empty away.

The Magnificat, from Luke 1:46f

What some Christians say:

The Catholic who is not a revolutionary is living in mortal sin. Camilo Torres

Over the last hundred years the Church has developed very clear guidelines and encouragement for all Catholics to come out into the open in order to work to make the world a more just, compassionate and peaceful place.

Bishop Brewer

The poverty of the poor is not a summons to alleviate their plight with acts of generosity, but rather a compelling obligation to fashion an entirely different social order.

Gustavo Gutierrez

Quick questions

1. Outline the work of Jaime Jaramilo.
   What do you find most impressive about his life?
2. Describe the different responses people might have to injustice.
   Which response do you consider is the best?
3. Was the Church wise to offer no support to Camilo Torres?

JAIME
JARAMILO
B. 1956.

CAMILO TORRES
B. 1930. D. 1966.

CHICO MENDES

> ***Chico had a lot of faith in God, and the Church always supported him. People hid him in church when enemies were after him.***
> **Chico's wife**

The ownership of land and the use or misuse of the earth's resources are the chief causes of injustice. Most wars are fought over land rights and the extension of borders. The civil war in El Salvador was caused by the unequal ownership of land; the entire country was owned by only fourteen wealthy families. Government forces, supported by American dollars, defended this élite against the poor, who continue to have no right of ownership at all.

Chico Mendes was a victim of similar injustice in Brazil. Francisco 'Chico' Alves Mendes was born in 1944 on the Cachoeira rubber estate, near Xapuri in North-West Brazil. He never went to school as this was forbidden by the land owners. At 9 years old he was working full-time as a rubber tapper. Landowners kept their workers illiterate so that they could cheat them in their wages. The workers were only allowed to shop in the estate shop, so they could never compare prices.

During the 1960s the rubber estates began to collapse when Southern cattle ranchers bought the land and felled the trees for pasture. The rubber tappers were brutally evicted from one estate after another. But in 1962 a stranger passed the Mendes home and stopped to talk to Chico. Although Chico could not read, he asked the stranger what was in the papers he held in his hand. Euclides Tavora was educated and working in the rubber industry; he was happy to share his knowledge and over the next few years he taught Chico to read. He also introduced him to the idea of trade unions to safeguard the rubber tappers' livelihood.

By 1968, when he was only 23, Chico felt ready to organise a union of workers in Xapuri, but it proved too difficult. In 1975 he was able to join a trade union group in Brasilia and he was made secretary. His friends, now more confident, began to join too. In Brasilia the Church leaders encouraged the movement and set up training days for the workers on church premises. Much encouraged, Chico returned home to Xapuri to try again in his local community. But his local priest, a friend of the landowners, was against all workers' organisations and he informed the police about Chico's union activities. From that time he was in constant danger.

Chico Mendes stood by his ideals and continued to protest against the massive deforestation by the landowners. His union members realised that they were not only fighting for social justice but also against environmental destruction. The unions developed the idea of '**empates**' – peaceful protests. Children walked in front at these gatherings to tell people it was a peaceful protest. But the landowners responded with violence and Chico was shot on 22 December 1988. He left a wife and two young children. His wife said: *'When Chico died I was filled with despair, but God comforted me and inspired me to carry on his work.'*

The Church in Brazil

Chico was let down by his local parish priest but supported by many Church leaders in Brazil. There will probably always be a struggle in the Church to identify how politically active a Christian should be. The Brazilian Church is very divided. Some bishops, like Chico's parish priest, totally oppose Liberation Theology, which encourages social action. Others champion the poor and have become their 'voice'. For many years Archbishop Helder Camara spoke out against the injustices. He once said, *'When God encounters injustice, oppression, exploitation, he takes sides. Then God and the Bible are subversive of such a situation.'* He is best known for his exclamation *'When I feed the hungry they call me a saint. When I ask why the people are hungry they call me a communist.'*

More recently, Cardinal Arns of Brazil has stood by the poor and spoken out against landowners and multinational corporations which cause environmental devastation. He said: *'We have to keep peace and social justice together with nature, because it is the only way humanity has to come to good development for the next millennium . . . In the last fifty years, the earth has been destroyed and devastated more than in all the millions of years behind us. If we want to live, and if we want to pass on something to the children, we have to do something immediately.'*

Rigoberta Menchu

The base communities in Latin America have inspired many women to take the lead in working for justice and human rights. No one has spoken out more clearly or more impressively than the 1992 Nobel Prize winner, Rigoberta Menchu. She is a poor *campesina* (country woman), a Mayan Indian from Guatemala, who until she was 19 spoke only K'iche. She was from a migrant family and worked as a maid. Today she is recognised internationally for her struggle to obtain human rights for the Mayan people who have been violently oppressed.

Rigoberta gained her courage and vision when she was trained as a parish catechist in the village of Chimel. The Spanish Sacred Heart Fathers encouraged her to learn Spanish and speak out for her people. She was motivated by her deep faith. She said: *'I am one who walks on the earth, not one who believes that the Kingdom of God comes only after death. Through all that I have experienced, through so much pain and suffering, I learned what the role of a committed Christian is, above all, to condemn and denounce injustices against the people.'*

The pain Rigoberta suffered is beyond belief. In 1979 her 16-year-old brother was kidnapped by soldiers, tortured and burnt alive in front of the family. In 1980, her father, Vicente, a union leader, took part in the occupation of the Spanish Embassy in Guatemala City following the massacre of Mayans. Police threw grenades into the building and her father was killed. Three months later, Rigoberta's mother was taken by soldiers, raped, mutilated and suffered a slow, agonising death under a soldier's guard – to prevent villagers from helping her. Rigoberta was hunted by the army and now has to live in exile in Mexico, where, supported by Maryknoll sisters, she works to draw attention to the violation of human rights of indigenous people throughout the Americas.

What the Scriptures say:

So God created human beings, making them in his own image. Genesis 1:27

What the Churches say:

Rights can be established on the basis of the doctrine of the image of God.
Church of England report, 1977

Quick questions

1. Describe the struggle for human rights in the Third World.
2. Who was Chico Mendes?
3. Who is Rigoberta Menchu?

CHICo
MENDES
B• 1944 • D • 1988 •

GUATEMALA
RIGOBERTA MENCHU
B 1959

SUMMARY ON JUSTICE

After thousands of years the human family has not learnt to share the earth's resources. Rather, because of greed and prejudice, the rich continue to get richer as the poor slip into deeper poverty.

In 1948 the UN adopted the Universal Declaration of Human Rights – a secular recognition of the dignity of each individual person. Jesus, inspired by the Book of Deuteronomy, had preached a similar call to justice when he told his disciples to love their neighbours as they loved themselves. This implied a willingness to share resources with others.

Today the Churches are taking this teaching very seriously. The Catholic Church has taken a positive Option for the Poor (an outcome of Liberation Theology). Organisations like CAFOD and Christian Aid, and countless individuals are working for greater justice.

GLOSSARY

Base communities	Active lay prayer groups who work for justice. Meetings begin with meditation on the Bible
CAFOD	Catholic Fund for Overseas Development. Agency set up in 1962 by Catholic bishops
CIIR	Catholic Institute for International Relations. Strong pressure group in RC Church for justice
Christian Aid	Largest Christian relief organisation. Set up by the Protestant Churches in 1945
Empates	Peaceful protests against injustice – where children walk in front of the marchers
Family Fast Day	Annual fund-raising campaign for CAFOD
Fundacion Niños de los Andes	Foundation set up by Jaime Jaramilo in Colombia to rehouse and support former street-children
Jubilee 2000	Movement calling for cancellation of world debt in celebration of the millennium
Liberation Theology	Recent theological insight that sees earthly freedom as the first stage of the coming of God's Kingdom. Christians must work for human rights
Option for the Poor	South American Catholic bishops' resolution at Medellin in 1968. Adopted by the whole Church
Tear Fund	The Evangelical Alliance Relief Fund supported by Cliff Richard

QUESTIONS

1. Write a paragraph on each of the following:
   (a) CAFOD
   (b) Christian Aid
   (c) Fundacion Niños de los Andes
   (d) Tear Fund

2. What is Liberation Theology?
   Why do you think it is not well received by all Christians?

3. Jesus said, 'Love your neighbour as you love yourself'.
   (a) Explain how this is really a call for justice.
   (b) Do you think that the Church should become political in working for human rights?

FEB 28, 1933.
ARBEIT
DIETRICH BONHOEFFER B. 1906. D. 1945.

SECTION 7: PEACE

Love your enemies and pray for those who persecute you.
Matthew 5:44

Introduction

One of the titles of Jesus is Prince of Peace. This section examines some of the ways Christians have worked for peace in the middle of hatred and war.

'As attested by all the cultures and civilisations the world has known, there is a principle of hope at work wherever people have lived . . . in spite of the fact that of the 3,400 years of recorded history, 3,166 were years of war and the remaining 234 were years of preparing for war.'

Leonardo Boff made this observation. He was aware that Christians are supported by their faith and hope in a God who, through Jesus, promised that peace will come with the Kingdom of God. People who work for peace bring about the Kingdom of God now, and they will be called God's own children. *'Blessed are those who work for peace; God will call them his children!'* Matthew 5:9.

Christians have always described God as *Love*. Where hatred and evil exist, God cannot be present. However, in every evil situation of war or injustice there are always individuals – like those described in this section of the book and countless others – who bring God and his Kingdom into the situation. They desire the good and determine to choose it. God is always in the GOOD.

DIETRICH BONHOEFFER

The Church must share in the secular problems of ordinary human life, not dominating, but helping and serving. It must tell people of every calling what it means to live in Christ, to exist for others.
Letters and Papers from Prison,
The Enlarged Edition, SCM Press, 1971

Young Dietrich Bonhoeffer had a wonderful childhood in Berlin. He was the sixth of eight children in a happy, comfortable, loving family. His father was a professor in psychiatry at the university. His mother managed the two family homes (one in the city, the other a holiday home in the country) and the servants. She was energetic and planned parties for the children, musical evenings and other entertainments, visits to interesting places and carefree holidays. Dietrich could spend hours in the large gardens or listen to the intelligent, educated adults who visited his parents. He was a healthy, robust boy and entered energetically into everything that was offered to him.

Professor Bonhoeffer taught his children good manners, ambition and correct behaviour. He was strict about correctness, especially in the way the children spoke. He said: *'Always say exactly what you mean; say only what you mean, and say it clearly.'* Everyone expected Dietrich to be a successful academic professor like his father. And their expectations were fulfilled, but to everyone's amazement it was as a professor of theology. The Bonhoeffer family had been **agnostic** (unwilling to say that God exists). Dietrich's scientist brother thought he was crazy to believe in God. But at Berlin University Dietrich emerged as a brilliant student of theology who could challenge his teachers, and leave them confused by the arguments he used.

The young theologian became a Lutheran pastor and continued his studies in New York. On returning to Germany he lectured at his old university. He rented rooms over an old bakery in a poor part of the city in order to help an old pastor teach some unruly boys in the parish. This experience taught Bonhoeffer that caring for people was what mattered. He had loved analysing the *idea* of God, now he found that God *as a living reality* mattered more. He said: *'God is more real than we are. He is not to be thought about like a thing, but met like a person. We ought to find out what God says and what he wants.'*

What Dietrich discovered, over the next few years, was that God wanted him to take the most shocking action a Christian pastor could ever imagine –

plotting to kill a person, Hitler. He was horrified at Hitler's rise to power in 1933, and the Nazi party's programme of **anti-Semitism**. Dietrich was in London at this time, trying to interpret events in Germany for other Europeans. When Hitler tried to get the Churches to serve his cause, Dietrich was recalled to Germany to train pastors who would oppose the new regime. They formed what was called the **Confessing Church**.

Dietrich was on a lecture tour of America when war was declared in 1939. He rushed home to share the anguish of his people. As the evils of Hitler's regime became a reality, Dietrich Bonhoeffer joined members of his family and other influential members of the German military in a plot to kill Hitler. He was a pacifist at heart (see page 108), but he believed that the death of this man could save the lives of thousands of innocent people. The plot was discovered, and Bonhoeffer was executed only days before the end of the war.

The events that led to Bonhoeffer's death

1933 Hitler elected chancellor. Deliberate steps taken to curtail people's freedom: trade unions banned, books burned in public, Jewish shops boycotted, many opponents to the regime murdered. Dietrich Bonhoeffer denounced Hitler on radio.

1934 Hitler attempted to get the backing of the Churches. He founded the **German Christian Movement**, under Nazi supervision. Bonhoeffer, with 2,000 pastors, founded the *Young Reformation Movement* (YRM) in protest. Some leading members imprisoned.

1935 The YRM grew to 800,000 members and took a new name, the Confessing Church, led by Martin Niemoller. Bonhoeffer chosen as rector of a seminary for training future pastors.

1937 Seminary closed down by the Gestapo. Bonhoeffer continued teaching and wrote *The Cost of Discipleship*. He insisted his students spend time daily in prayer and meditation on Scripture.

1939 Bonhoeffer returned from America as war was declared. Became disillusioned with the Confessing Church for its cowardice; many members were joining the army, claiming Hitler had improved their lives. Dietrich insisted that better food and employment was a bribe to obtain support for an evil regime that aimed to make Germans the 'Master Race'.

1940 Bonhoeffer banned from preaching. He and his brother-in-law, Hans von Dohnanyi, joined high-ranking military men in a conspiracy to kill Hitler. Their headquarters were in the Government Security Department, the Abwehr.

1942 Bonhoeffer part of Operation U7, to help prominent Jews escape to Switzerland. Other undercover activities in Europe.

1943 First bomb attempt on Hitler failed. Hans and Dietrich were arrested on 5 April and taken to Tegel prison. Dietrich began writing notes on scraps of paper smuggled in. Decided to commit suicide rather than break under interrogation, but found it unnecessary since he was able to confuse his interrogators.

1944 More attempts on Hitler's life by other conspirators. All fail. Bonhoeffer confined to Gestapo headquarters in Berlin's Prince Albrecht Strasse.

1945 Bonhoeffer taken to Buchenwald concentration camp. Transferred to Flossenburg in April, and executed by hanging a few days later.

The importance of Bonhoeffer

A British officer in prison with Bonhoeffer wrote of him: *'Happiness and joy radiated from him, he was calm, normal, perfectly at his ease. His God was real and close to him.'* It is remarkable that Dietrich achieved such serenity when he had to make terrible decisions, and suffer for them. His life shows how costly it is to be a disciple of Christ. The letters he sent to family and friends were collected and published as *Letters and Papers from Prison*. His writings show compassion, deep faith, and humour.

Bonhoeffer's experiences made him rethink the basics of Christian faith and ethical behaviour. His writings, though undeveloped, have influenced all post-war theology. He proposed a 'religionless Christianity' – a radical theological stand, based on his understanding that God influences the world from a position of weakness, not power. *'God lets himself be pushed out of the world on to the cross. God would have us know that we must live as people who manage our lives without him.'* He called this *'the coming of age of Christians'.*

Quick questions

1. Briefly outline Dietrich Bonhoeffer's life (about 150 words).
2. Why did Bonhoeffer support the Confessing Church?
3. Why did Bonhoeffer take part in the conspiracy against Hitler?
4. Do you think it can ever be right to kill another person?

FRANZ JAEGERSTAETTER

I can only congratulate you on this country-man of yours who lived as a saint and now dies a hero. I say with certainty that this simple man is the only saint that I have ever met in my lifetime.

Father Jochmann to some Austrian nuns, 9 August 1943

In 1917, in a small village called St Radegund in Upper Austria, a local farmer married a young woman who already had an illegitimate son, Franz. They became the Jaegerstaetter family. Young Franz went to the village school until he was 14, then joined his father on the farm. He is still remembered by the oldest inhabitants of the village as a member of their local gang. He was cheerful and boisterous, he took part in the regular 'battles' against neighbouring village boys, and he spent much of his youth in and out of the village inn and with the local girls. Everyone in the village attended church, but Franz admitted later that his Christianity was only 'half-baked'.

Not very much is known about Franz. He continued working on the farm for most of his life, with a break of two years when he disappeared to work in some iron mines. Rumour had it that this coincided with the unexplained pregnancy of a local girl. He returned to the village sporting a new motorcycle, the first seen in that part of Austria. In 1936 Franz married and the young husband, influenced by a devoutly Christian wife, changed his attitude towards religion. He took his faith more seriously and became sacristan in the church, working closely with an independently minded priest. He was influenced by a cousin who had joined a fundamentalist biblical sect; it encouraged him to study the Bible for himself and to discuss it freely.

In 1938 Hitler took over Austria. Franz and his wife were deeply disturbed by the brutality and ideology of the Nazi regime. Franz was the only one in the village to vote against the take-over. This made him suspect and highly unpopular. Because he was a farmer he could defer compulsory military service, which he did twice. Over the next few years the couple had three daughters and lived quietly together in what Franz later wrote was a time 'of joy and many graces'. On 25 February 1943 he was ordered to report to the recruiting centre for the German army at Enns. As he left the village a neighbour shouted, *'God go with you, Franz'*. He received a strange reply: *'You will see no more of me.'* Franz had no intention of joining up for military service and he knew his refusal meant death. He was beheaded in a Berlin prison, six months later.

Franz Jaegerstaetter was a very ordinary brave man who refused to compromise with his conscience. He believed Hitler's war was unjust and brutal. His Christian faith led him to believe it would be wrong to take part in it. What is remarkable is that he refused to accept the well-meaning advice of priests and his bishop that he should change his mind for the sake of his family. He wrote lovingly to his wife and spent his prison days in prayer and in small acts of thoughtfulness for the other prisoners. One of the prison chaplains wrote of him: *'Not for an instant did I ever entertain the notion that Jaegerstaetter was a "fanatic" or even mentally deranged. He did not give the slightest impression of being so. I was far more inclined to marvel at his bravery and his simple, deep and genuine piety.'*

What the Scriptures say:

Thou shalt not kill. Exodus 20:13, KJB

One of Jesus' companions reached for his sword . . . 'Put your sword back in its place', Jesus said to him, 'All who take the sword will die by the sword.' Matthew 26:51-52

Conscientious objection to war

Franz Jaegerstaetter stands in a long line of Christians who have refused to take part in war. There were many others in prison with him for this reason. It is not clear whether he was a total pacifist (see below) or whether he just objected to Hitler's war.

Conscientious objection had become an issue during the First World War. Objectors in Britain were imprisoned and treated harshly. Even after the war, they continued to be targets for discrimination. By the time of the war against Hitler, conscientious objection had won some recognition in Britain, and objectors were offered other forms of service. Even so, **Amnesty International** report that hundreds of young people across the world continue to be imprisoned – even in countries like France and Finland – because of their refusal to perform military service on the grounds of conscience. The Church has consistently called for universal acceptance of this human right.

Amnesty International

This independent pressure group was founded in 1961 by a British lawyer, Peter Benenson. As a network of voluntary groups and individuals, it campaigns for the release of prisoners of conscience. Amnesty works in an impartial way to uphold the rights of individuals who are condemned by reason of their beliefs, ethnic origin, colour or gender. Amnesty opposes torture and the death penalty, hostage-taking and arbitrary killings. In 1977 Amnesty International received the Nobel Peace Prize for *'its efforts on behalf of defending human dignity against violence and subjugation'.*

Pacifism

A pacifist is someone who believes that war can never be justified; that it is morally wrong. Until the fourth century most Christians were pacifist, claiming that Jesus did not fight, even in self-defence, and that he called his disciples to live in total peace: *'Peace is what I leave with you; it is my own peace that I give you'* (John 14:27). But others claimed that Jesus defended the rights of people who were unjustly treated, and that he was at times vigorous in his actions: *'Do not think that I have come to bring peace to the world. I did not come to bring peace, but a sword'* (Matthew 10:34).

By the fifth century Augustine of Hippo was claiming that war could sometimes be justified as the 'lesser of two evils'. This laid the foundation for the **Just War theory**. But pacifism remained a strong ideal in Christianity. Many joined monasteries rather than fight in the Crusades. In the early fifteenth century Jan Hus founded the pacifist Moravian Brethren in Prague. The Quakers, founded by George Fox in the seventeenth century, have suffered persistent persecution for their total pacifism.

Summary

1907 Franz born in St Radegund

1917 His mother married and took the name Jaegerstaetter

1921 Franz left school. Worked on the farm

1936 Married

1938 Refused to support Hitler's take-over of Austria

1943 Called to military service
Refused. Executed

Quick questions

1. Write a short description of Franz Jaegerstaetter's life.
2. What is the difference between conscientious objection and pacifism?
3. How can the Christian Churches accept the Just War theory?

REI
Lieber Vater
komm bald
LINZ
FRANZ
JAEGERSTAETTER
B. 1909. D. 1943.

ULSTER
CONNAUGHT
LEINSTER
MUNSTER
DAVID TRIMBLE
B. 1944
JOHN HUME
B. 1937

DAVID TRIMBLE and JOHN HUME

In 1998 the Catholic John Hume and the Protestant David Trimble, members of opposing parties in Northern Ireland, received the Nobel Peace Prize. It was recognition for the remarkable movement towards a peace solution for Ireland that had resulted in the Good Friday Agreement.

The movement began thirteen years earlier in 1985 with an **Anglo-Irish Agreement** by which the Catholic Republic of Ireland was given a consultative role in the government of the Protestant Ulster Province. The agreement did not last very long as both sides have different aspirations. The Catholics want a united Ireland but Protestant Ulster wants to remain separate from the Republic, and united with England.

Twenty years before, when two brave women were calling for peace (see page 112), and Ian Paisley was shouting them down, John Hume was also an isolated voice calling for tolerance and reconciliation. Today it is Paisley who is the isolated voice, and Hume is recognised as the visionary who has overcome prejudice and hatred by his patient insistence on a non-violent search for unity. Hume, of the SDLP (Social Democratic Liberal Party), was praised by the Nobel chairman: *'More than anyone else, Mr Hume is the architect behind the peace process and the solution chosen in the Good Friday Agreement. He has had to swallow sometimes very harsh criticism from within his own ranks as well as from others. He has stood firm and his policy has won through.'*

David Trimble is a more aggressive politician, leader of the Ulster Unionist Party. It is seen as quite extraordinary that he could encourage a majority of Unionists to enter an agreement with the opposition Catholics. It took remarkable courage to risk alienation from his own party; but he managed to remove some of the fear and suspicion that has existed for centuries between different parties in Ireland. He remains very cautious. *'We will go on all the better if we walk rather than run'*, he said when he received the prize. The Good Friday Agreement seemed only a promise of peace with many obstacles still in the way.

But on the morning of 2 December 1999 the people of Northern Ireland woke up to the momentous reality that twenty-five years of direct rule from London was over. At midnight power had been transferred from Westminster to Stormont. People who had opposed each other so fiercely started work together in a new partnership administration, led by David Trimble, Northern Ireland's First Minister. The new peace stumbled almost immediately; old fears refused to die. But the majority still hope and pray for a permanent peace.

Hume and Trimble received the Peace Prize, but there are other people whose ideals and commitment to peace contributed to the signing of the original agreement. History will record the part played by Tony Blair and Mo Mowlam for the British government, and by Bertie Ahern and Gerry Adams, Catholic leaders who managed to tame the IRA.

Christian Unity

Bitter rivalry and contempt has turned Christian against Christian throughout the ages. Such divisions are a scandal. It is easy to see why so many people turn their back on religion. In 1910 some Protestant ministers in Edinburgh vowed to look at the denominations more positively. They agreed to concentrate on the many things which all Christian denominations have in common, such as

- allegiance to Jesus Christ
- the Bible
- the historic Creeds
- Baptism
- Eucharist.

In 1940, the French Père Couturier took a further step and suggested that Christians prayed together. By 1948 a **World Council of Churches** was formed. In the 1960s Pope John XXIII encouraged Roman Catholics to enter this new dialogue. In recent years the Catholic and Anglican Churches have entered into serious theological discussion together. This forward movement of the Churches is known as **Ecumenism**. It does not imply the formation of a single, uniform Church but asks Christians to respect denominations other than their own. It encourages them to work for that unity among Christians for which Christ prayed. He said unity should be a sign of his followers.

What the Scriptures say:

I pray that they may all be one. Father! May they be in us, just as you are in me and I am in you. May they be one, so that the world will believe that you sent me. John 17:21

The purpose of all war is peace.

St Augustine

Where peace is, God is.

George Herbert

EARLIER HISTORY

The illustrations on pages 110 and 113 show four people who have received the Nobel Peace Prize for their efforts to bring an end to violence in Ulster, Northern Ireland. The history of Ireland is complicated, right from the fifth century BC when it was invaded by Celtic tribes. These tribes divided the island into warring kingdoms. Today their boundaries still mark out the four provinces – which are further broken up into counties.

The main religious troubles began during the seventeenth-century Reformation. England, now largely Protestant, asserted its rule over Ireland by sending English and Scottish settlers to the northern province of Ulster (the *Plantation of Ulster*, 1610), where they took over six of its nine counties (see map). Ireland, still almost entirely Catholic, rebelled, and the revolt was not put down till 1650 when Oliver Cromwell crossed the sea to suppress it.

Under the Stuart kings, the Irish revolt re-emerged, especially when James II proclaimed himself a Catholic. England immediately rejected him in favour of his daughter Mary, who married the Dutch Protestant William of Orange. In 1690 William crossed the sea and defeated the Irish followers of James II in the Battle of the Boyne.

There followed a century of Irish struggles for freedom, and English suppression. In 1801 the *Act of Union* reasserted English control of Ireland. But the enormous suffering in the country (the 1846 *potato famine* reduced the population by half) won widespread support for independence and *Home Rule*. This was finally achieved in 1921, when the Catholic South (Irish Free State, later called Republic of Ireland, or Eire) was made independent of the mainly Protestant province of Ulster, which chose to remain united to England. The division has caused continual violence with terrorist outrages from both the Republicans (led by the IRA) and the Protestant Ulster Unionists.

MAIREAD CORRIGAN *and* BETTY WILLIAMS

In 1968 serious trouble began in Northern Ireland when Roman Catholics claimed they were discriminated against in housing and employment. British troops were sent in to restore peace and protect the Catholic minority. In 1972 the parliament at Stormont was taken over by direct rule from Westminster. But violence continued. Mairead lost three young relatives, mown down by a car after an IRA driver was shot. Betty Williams saw it happen. Her father was a Protestant and her mother a Catholic. The two women decided to work together against the violence and formed the **Peace People**. They attracted thousands to their rallies, calling on women, saying: *'Let all women encourage men to have the courage not to turn up for war.'* Mairead and Betty received the Nobel Prize in 1977 for their efforts in the face of great provocation. The IRA threatened them; Ian Paisley, a Protestant religious and political leader, treated them with contempt.

The 'Peace People' did not last. Under such stress Mairead and Betty even fell out with each other. But even though worse violence took place in the 1980s and 90s, a seed had been sown. There is recognition today that the genuine courage shown by the two women did have a lasting effect, and contributed to the 1998 historic *Good Friday Agreement*.

BETTY
WILLIAMS
B. 1943
MAIREAD
CORRIGAN
B. 1944

MARY
McALEESE
B. 1951
DUBLIN

MARY McALEESE

She writes with the authority of a woman who has herself suffered from sectarian violence but who has been actively involved for many years in the search for peace in Northern Ireland. **from the blurb, *Reconciled Being: Love in Chaos***

Mary McAleese was elected President of Ireland in 1997. She is a remarkable woman of deep religious faith. A Roman Catholic who was born in Belfast, her parents had nine children and the family suffered in the sectarian violence to the extent that they lost their home and the family business. It was this suffering that made Mary more determined than ever to look for ways of reconciliation rather than bitterness and blame. She probably owes her determination to her mother. When she was a teenager, she told the parish priest who was visiting her parents that she wanted to become a lawyer. The priest said: *'You can't because you are a woman, and no one in your family is in law.'* To Mary's amazement her mother, who was normally deeply respectful of all priests, roared at him: *'You – out!'* and to Mary: *'You ignore him.'*

Mary did indeed ignore the priest. She graduated in Law from Queen's University, Belfast, where she is now Pro Vice-Chancellor. For twelve years she lectured in Law at Trinity College, Dublin, and she has also been a journalist. She is married and has three children. It is from her love of family life that she draws inspiration for her involvement in the search for peace in Northern Ireland. She is also at the heart of the Catholic Church's debate over the role of women. In her writings and her lectures, Mary often uses her personal life as illustrations for her ideas. In 1997 she was invited to give *The John Main Seminar*, an annual event in memory of the Benedictine priest who revived an early tradition of meditation prayer. Her lectures at the seminar are published in the book, *Reconciled Being: Love in Chaos*. It is a witness to her life of deep faith and prayer. She explores the origins of violence, and maps out the painful path of reconciliation. She points out that conflict may well be genetically programmed – in each one of us from the start. She recalls an incident when her twins were only two years old. They shared a bedroom and to get them to sleep she would turn out the light. *'But by some miracle it always turned itself on again.'* Mary waited outside the door and listened to the children.

Sara to Justin: 'Justin, turn on the light.'
Justin, saint and self-preservationist: 'No, Mammy will be cross.'
'Turn it on or I won't be your friend.'
'No, Mammy will be very cross.'
'Justin, turn the light on or I am going to thump you.'
Light goes on. Enter Mother.
'Who turned on the light?'
Sara: 'He did.'

Mary patiently taught her own children to replace this inclination to violence and blame with tolerance and love. She has been able to inspire countless others to the same generosity by her professional life and witness. She always turns to her faith in God as the source of her convictions. She quotes Mother Teresa, saying Christians *'should give until it hurts'*, and she goes on to say: *'This has to be right, doesn't it, for the cross of Christ is the ultimate form of giving until it hurts, self-giving to the point of total self-abandonment to the other, especially if they are on the other side.'*

Corrymeela

Mary McAleese stands for the countless people in Ireland, North and South of the border, Protestant and Catholic, men and women, young and old, who desire peace and reconciliation. Some of these people turn to their religious faith as support. In 1965, as the unrest in Northern Ireland became serious, a community for reconciliation was set up in Corrymeela on the County Antrim coast at Ballycastle. Protestants and Catholics chose to live together in harmony and peace, offering this as an example of what is possible – when God is at the heart of community.

Today Corrymeela has grown into a large centre for peace, renewal and healing. The campus houses a resident team and room for over 100 visitors at any one time. Young people go for training weekends; other groups include pensioners, prisoners' wives, handicapped people and it is often a sanctuary for victims of the 'troubles' in the province. In the summer many volunteers from Ireland and abroad go to work and pray with the visitors. The Corrymeela ideal has spread beyond Ballycastle; smaller, local ecumenical groups meet to build up trust and co-operation.

What the Churches say:

There is something of God – the seed of the spirit – in all people. Quakers believe that more can be accomplished by appealing to this capacity for love and goodness, in ourselves and in others, than can be hoped for by threatening punishment or retaliation if people behave badly.

Quaker Peace Testimony

Quick questions

1. Outline the cause of sectarian trouble in Northern Ireland.
2. Write a paragraph about each of the following people: John Hume, David Trimble and Mary McAleese.
3. Write a description of the Corrymeela Community.

SUMMARY ON PEACE

It is a sad fact that wars continue to be fought all the time. Some are headline news and involve several nations. Others are restless civil conflicts that stretch on for years and are no longer reported. Christians are not agreed about the justification for war. Some claim Jesus was a pacifist. The Quaker movement has adopted this view.

However, the main body of the Christian Church has accepted (even helped to formulate) the Just War theory. Alongside this the Churches remind Christians that Jesus preached peace and tolerance. The struggle to reconcile a call to peace and the need to fight evil is a matter of conscience for individuals.

Dietrich Bonhoeffer put aside his pacifism to help plot the overthrow of Hitler; whilst Franz Jaegerstaetter chose execution rather than join the army. The Gospel does not have clear answers to moral dilemmas.

GLOSSARY

Agnostic	One who believes that nothing can be known of God's existence
Amnesty International	Pressure group founded in 1961 by Peter Benenson to campaign for release of prisoners of conscience
Anglo-Irish Agreement	1985 resolution which gave the Republic of Ireland (Catholic) a consultative role in the government of the Protestant Ulster Province
Anti-Semitism	Prejudice and hostility towards Jews
Confessing Church	Church formed by pastors (led by Niemoller) to oppose Hitler's regime
Ecumenism	Wider movement of church co-operation and unity
German Christian Movement	Founded by Hitler in an attempt to get support from the Churches
Just War Theory	Conditions universally accepted as justifying war
Peace People	Movement for peace founded by two women in Northern Ireland in the 1970s
World Council of Churches	Formed in 1948 to introduce dialogue between Churches

QUESTIONS

1. (a) Outline the reasons why people go to war.
   (b) Select a number of biblical texts that call for peace, not war.
2. What is a pacifist?
   Describe the life of a Christian pacifist who died for his beliefs.
3. (a) Do you think there can ever be a 'Just War'? Use real examples to back up your view.
   (b) Show how others might disagree with your point of view.

STEPHEN
FIRST CENTURY A.D

SECTION 8: TAKE UP YOUR CROSS

Whoever does not carry his own cross . . .
cannot be my disciple.

Luke 14:27

Introduction

Many men and women have given their lives for the truth, following the example of Jesus. They are **martyrs** – that is, they have 'borne witness' to the point of death, to show that they share Jesus' understanding of God. This section looks at two early Christian martyrs and two from the twentieth century.

From the early days of the Church Christians have paradoxically claimed that the most important moment in the drama of Jesus was his death. They call the day on which he died *Good* Friday. (Christian belief in the Resurrection is in no way meant to underrate the importance of his death). The Gospel writers saw the cross as the crucial test of faithfulness to God. Jesus died because he refused to compromise. He would not take the easy way out by changing his teaching to suit the authorities. He showed that human values have to give way for God's Kingdom to be established on earth.

Followers of Jesus can expect to be treated as he was. Discipleship is costly. A Nicaraguan priest, Fr Miguel D'Escoto, recognised that 'taking up the cross' is demanding when he wrote: *'I don't think we Christians have understood what carrying the cross means. We are not carrying the cross when we are poor or sick or suffering small everyday things – these are all part of life. The cross comes when we try to change things. That is how it came for Jesus.'*

ST STEPHEN

Feast: 26 December

Now Stephen, a man full of God's grace and power, did great wonders and miraculous signs among the people. Opposition arose, however, from members of the Synagogue of the Freedmen. **Acts 6:8-9**

Stephen is the first martyr: the first disciple to die for his faith in Jesus. All we know about him is found in chapters six and seven of the Acts of the Apostles, written by Luke. In the very early days of the Church, the apostles chose seven deacons to assist them in their work. Luke says that the first of these seven was Stephen, *'a man full of God's grace and power'*. It is thought that Stephen was a Greek-speaking Jew, because the deacons were asked to look after Greek-speaking widows in the Jerusalem Christian community.

Stephen was an enthusiastic preacher, very anxious to share the Good News that Jesus had proclaimed. His enthusiastic words angered the Jews of Cyrene, Alexandria and Cilicia – a group known as the *Synagogue of the Freedmen*. They accused Stephen of blasphemy against Moses and God. The authorities were notified and Stephen was called before the Sanhedrin (Jewish Council). Stephen addressed the Council at length, outlining the history of Israel and accusing his hearers of being stiff-necked. *'You always resist the Holy Spirit'*, he said, *'and now you have betrayed and murdered the Holy One.'* This infuriated the Council who had Stephen dragged from the city and stoned to death.

What the Scriptures say:

While they were stoning him, Stephen prayed, 'Lord Jesus, receive my spirit'. Then he fell on his knees and cried out, 'Lord, do not hold this sin against them'. When he had said this, he fell asleep. Acts 7:59-60, NIV

When they came to the place called 'the Skull', there they crucified him . . . Jesus said, 'Forgive them, Father! They don't know what they are doing.' . . . Jesus called out with a loud voice, 'Father, into your hands I place my spirit'. He said this and died. Luke 23:33-34, 46

Martyrdom

Martyrs are those people who suffer and die for their beliefs. There are political martyrs, like suicide bombers and hunger strikers who starve to death to make a statement about their ideals. Others die for the sake of upholding high moral standards of behaviour, like Franz Jaegerstaetter, who died rather than fight in an immoral war. Across the centuries, thousands of men and women have died rather than deny their religious beliefs, or compromise their faith.

The Christian Church is described as being 'founded on the blood of the martyrs'. This is because in the early centuries Christians faced persecution and countless numbers died for their belief in Jesus. This is still happening today in many countries, such as the Sudan, parts of Indonesia and Latin America. Luke describes the earliest persecutions in the **Acts of the Apostles.** His description of Stephen's death is interesting. You can see from the two texts above that Luke sees Stephen's death as an echo of the death of Jesus.

There are many stories written of martyrdoms: beheadings, stonings, gruesome tortures leading to agonising deaths. Some of the worst accounts come from the religious persecutions in England during the Reformation. Protestants and Catholics were brutal to each other. People flocked to see Catholic prisoners hung, drawn and quartered in London, after they had been dragged on hurdles through the streets. Catholics flocked to see Protestants burnt to death.

The best known of the English Catholic martyrs is **St Thomas More**. He was a man with a brilliant career – a lawyer at Lincoln's Inn, an author and scholar of international repute, a member of Parliament, Speaker of the House of Commons, an ambassador for England and Lord Chancellor in King Henry VIII's reign. He was known for his love of family life, his deep spirituality, his good humour and solid commonsense. Everything was going well for him until King Henry broke with Rome over his divorce. Thomas More had to choose between loyalty to his king or loyalty to his faith. He chose his faith and was beheaded on Tower Hill in 1535. Thomas More went to his death with a gentleness and joy that is characteristic of all the martyrs. He joked with the guard: *'See me safely up the scaffold. My coming down I can see to myself.'* He told the crowd, *'I am the King's good servant, but God's first'.*

Thomas Cranmer is often thought of as a scheming politician because of his influence on Henry VIII and his use of the political happenings of the time. He was originally a convinced Roman Catholic. The pope made him Grand Penitentiary of England in 1532. A year later he received a royal summons to become Archbishop of Canterbury. But at this time he was carefully considering the ideas of reformers in Europe and changing his ideas. In 1549 Thomas Cranmer piloted a prayer book in English, more than 400 years before the Roman Catholic Church caught up. Between 1549 and 1552 he had many discussions with continental reformers, and produced the *Book of Common Prayer*, which is still widely used in the Church of England and is the basis of all common prayer in the Anglican Communion.

When Mary was on the throne Cranmer was burned to death for refusing to go back on the reforms which had been made. With his fellow bishops, Latimer and Ridley, he suffered bravely, putting his hand (which had written so much) first into the flames.

Quick questions

1. Write 100 words about St Stephen.
2. Write 100 words about St Thomas More.
3. Write 100 words about Archbishop Cranmer.
4. What does it mean to say *'the Church is built on the blood of martyrs'*?
5. There are no longer persecutions and martyrdoms in England. Why not?

THOMAS CRANMER
B. 1489.
D. 1556.
THOMAS MORE
B. 1478. D. 1535.
2001

Εἴ τις θέλει ὀπίσω μου ἐλθεῖν, ἀπαρνησάσθω ἑαυτὸν καὶ ἀράτω τὸν σταυρὸν αὐτοῦ, καὶ ἀκολουθείτω μοι.

Literal translation :
If anyone wants to come after me, let him deny himself,
and let him take up his cross, and let him follow me.

Authorised Version :
Whosoever will come after me,
let him deny himself,
and take up his cross,
and follow me.

New World Version :
If you want to help me
you must give all your heart to it,
you must put yourself last.
you must be ready to
let people do their worst to you.
And you must keep your eyes on me.

New English Version :
Anyone who wishes
to be a follower of mine
must leave himself behind;
he must take up his cross,
and come with me.

Jerusalem Version:
If anyone wants to be
a follower of mine,
let him renounce himself,
and take up his cross,
and follow me.

ST MARK

Feast: 25 April

> *Mark . . . the model of all who work for God unnoticed . . . We can hear him saying in his own blunt way: 'Don't look at me, look at Him.'*
>
> ***The Saints*, edited by John Coulson**

Most biblical scholars are agreed that Mark was the first of the four **evangelists** to write a Gospel. He wrote after AD 64 when Rome was burnt down. It became a difficult time for the Christians living in Rome. Nero blamed them for the troubles and had them sent to the lions in the Colosseum. Mark was not surprised at this persecution. After all, a Christian was a disciple (follower) of Jesus who was put to death under Roman law. If disciples were really following his example and teaching they had to expect martyrdom. Tradition has it that Mark himself was martyred during the reign of the Emperor Trajan. Mark is most especially remembered in Venice, where his relics (taken there in 829 from Alexandria) are said to be buried beneath the high altar in the magnificent church of San Marco.

Mark is thought to have been the companion of Peter, one of the closest friends of Jesus. About AD 100, the scholar Papias wrote that: *'The Elder* [probably an earlier disciple] *used to say that Mark, who had been the interpreter of Peter, wrote down accurately all that Peter remembered of what the Lord* [Jesus] *said and did, though not in order.'* From references about a disciple called Mark made in letters from Paul and Peter, and in Luke's *Acts of the Apostles*, it is assumed that the Gospel writer is John Mark, the son of Mary, who gave shelter to Peter when he was released from prison. Mark accompanied Paul and Barnabas on their first missionary journey. In a letter Peter calls Mark his 'son', so perhaps Peter baptised his family. It is believed that Peter died in about AD 65; maybe his death as a martyr inspired Mark to write his Gospel. He could see in Peter what it meant to be a true disciple of Jesus.

Mark wrote in a simple, popular Greek – the literary language of the Roman Empire. He introduced some Aramaic and Latin words into his writings. This suggests he was a Jew who spoke Aramaic, and that he lived in a Roman environment. His Greek is not very good, but his writing style is wonderfully descriptive and powerful. Mark would have made a good popular journalist.

Against the Roman background of conflict and persecution, Mark collected some of the traditional stories about Jesus and put them together in a coherent narrative. The main focus of the Gospel is the account of Jesus' death. The first thirteen chapters of the Gospel are an introduction to the last three, where he describes the last days of Jesus' life and briefly mentions the resurrection. The thirteen chapters set the scene for the end of the story. Mark, knowing the dramatic end of Jesus' life, selected very carefully stories and events that would unfold the drama and reveal the true identity of Jesus. He calls him the Son of God on page one, but then seems to hide his identity as a great secret. He wants his readers to keep asking for themselves, 'Who is he?'

It is very clear that the Gospel is not a biography. It is Mark's way of sharing his faith with other Christians. They needed reassuring, in the midst of such persecution, that Jesus really was the Messiah.

An outline of the Gospel

1. **The prologue**
   The opening verse sets the scene. *'The beginning of the Gospel of Jesus Christ, the Son of God.'* Mark says exactly who Jesus is. He describes how Jesus
   - is proclaimed by John the Baptist
   - is anointed by the Spirit
   - is the One who does battle with Satan.
2. **Preaching in parables**
   Mark shows Jesus as a Jewish teacher using parables to challenge the crowds. Stories capture the imagination and linger on in the memory. Jesus described the Kingdom of God in his stories. Twenty years later Luke developed this image of Jesus as teacher, by including many more parables.
3. **The miracles of Jesus**
   Jesus worked marvels for people in need: the sick, the blind, the lame. Miracle stories were significant for Mark because they witnessed to the power of God working in Jesus. The rule of God was replacing the rule of Satan. Mark shows the battle going on between God and Satan.
4. **Conflict in the Gospel**
   Mark presents a Jesus who is fearless in confronting authority. The Gospel is full of conflict situations. Mark shows that the real authority lay in Jesus' teaching, for he spoke on God's behalf. Mark explains how this led to his death.

5. The passion and death of Jesus
Mark saw Jesus' death as the inevitable end of someone determined to confront a world in the grip of Satan. The cross was the final test of Jesus' faithfulness to God and opposition to Satan.

6. The resurrection
The resurrection is the touchstone of Christian faith. A Christian believes that Jesus lives on after his death, that his death is not the end of the story, but its beginning. Mark's story of the resurrection conveys the bewilderment of the women, first desolate and then awestruck.

Strangely, however, Mark's account ends with the women too terrified to *'go, tell his disciples . . .* [Jesus] *is going ahead of you'*, as they had been instructed by the young man at the tomb. They lack courage. Mark suggests that Jesus always goes on ahead and asks his disciples to follow. He urges his persecuted readers to follow Jesus. It is never too late.

What the Scriptures say:

> *They were on their way up to Jerusalem, with Jesus leading the way, and the disciples were astonished, while those who followed were afraid . . . 'We are going up to Jerusalem,' he said, 'and the Son of Man will be betrayed to the chief priests and teachers of the law. They will condemn him to death.'* Mark 10:32-33, NIV

Summary

- Mark was a Jew
- He wrote in clumsy Greek
- His descriptions are vivid
- He was a friend of Peter
- He wrote for Christians in Rome who were undergoing persecution
- His theme is the mystery of Jesus
- He explores a battle between God and Satan

Quick questions

1. Who was Mark?
2. Describe the background, in Rome, to his writing.
3. Look up Mark 10:52. Why is the sentence *. . . immediately he followed Jesus along the road* [to Jerusalem] significant?

ST MAXIMILIAN KOLBE

Feast: 14 August

Each time I saw Father Kolbe in the courtyard [of Auschwitz] I felt within myself an extraordinary effusion of his goodness.
Father Rusczak, fellow prisoner

On 14 August 1941, Maximilian Kolbe, prisoner no.16670, died in Auschwitz concentration camp from an injection of carbolic acid. His name was not always Maximilian. He had been baptised Raymond, the second son of a poor Polish family. They came from Zdunska Wola, where his father was a weaver of cloth. His parents were extraordinarily devout Catholics who taught the children to love Jesus and Mary before anything else. Raymond was, from a very early age, captivated by the idea of martyrdom. He even dreamt about it.

The boys entered the junior seminary in Lwow where Raymond showed signs of a brilliant future in science and mathematics. Strangely, for a religious boy, he also became patriotically enthusiastic about the army and nearly abandoned the idea of priesthood for a military career. His parents seem to have influenced him otherwise and in 1910, aged 16, he became a Franciscan novice and took the name Maximilian. The Franciscans, recognising the student's brilliance, sent him to Rome in 1912 where he stayed for seven years studying philosophy and theology. He was ordained priest in 1918, and left Rome the following year, just as Poland gained its independence.

Maximilian never lost his enthusiasm for fighting, but he made his 'battleground' a spiritual one – the war between good and evil. As a young priest he set about founding an 'army of crusaders' who would fight for goodness. Maximilian threw his whole being into spreading his beliefs throughout the country. He did this by becoming an expert in the media. He pioneered a number of new magazines and newspapers *'to illuminate the truth and show the true way to happiness'*. He was so successful that in 1927 the Franciscans had to build an enormous monastery, Niepokalanov, to house his work. By this time he was suffering from TB, yet his enthusiasm and love for Mary had become 'infectious' and hundreds of men were joining the Franciscans. By 1939 his monastery had 762 members – priests, brothers and seminarians. He was even publishing a daily Catholic newspaper.

Meanwhile, in spite of failing health, Maximilian wanted to follow Francis' example and go to mission lands. In 1930 he went to Nagasaki in Japan and set up a monastery there. He was invited to teach philosophy at the seminary in exchange for permission to print his newspapers. Maximilian showed great insight in Japan. He did not impose Christianity; he respected Buddhism and Shintoism, seeking ways for dialogue. The Franciscans are still respected in Nagasaki today. Maximilian studied Russian in the hopes of starting a foundation in Moscow and initiating a dialogue with Communism, but he was recalled to Poland in 1936. He was a very sick man, racked with violent headaches, but he was to continue his religious journalism for a few more years until his death in the concentration camp.

Imprisonment and death

As war was approaching Father Maximilian began to prepare his priests and the people of Poland by encouraging them to accept suffering with love. He reminded them that Mary understood what suffering was for she had stood at the foot of the cross. After the war, the Polish bishops declared that their nation had been prepared to endure and survive the horrors of the war by the work of the Franciscan priest. He was responsible for the revival of religious faith in Poland.

By September 1939 the work at Niepokalanov was stopped by the invading Germans. The Franciscans were deported to Germany but released three months later. On his return Maximilian organised shelters for Polish refugees, most of them Jewish. He said, *'Our mission is among them in the days that lie ahead'.* But in 1941 Fr Maximilian provoked his own arrest by publishing his newspaper again. He wrote again of his conviction that the only battlefield was a personal, inner one, between sin and love. He was arrested and sent to Pawiak prison in Warsaw before deportation to Auschwitz. All witnesses attest that the Franciscan priest was treated with exceptional cruelty. He was beaten, forced to carry the heaviest tree trunks on work patrols, kicked and lashed. He never lost his serenity and spoke only of God's love to his fellow prisoners. He shared his thin ration of soup or bread with others, and always took the back of the queue.

This example drew other prisoners to listen in secret to his words, right up to the end. It came for him in August. On 31 July three prisoners escaped, one from his block, Block 14A. In reprisal, the Lagerfuhrer picked ten prisoners from the block and sent them to the underground starvation cell. When one of them cried out, *'O my poor wife, my poor children! I shall never see them again'*, Maximilian stepped forward and offered to take his place. The guard accepted and the Franciscan priest joined the group. An eye-witness attests that over the next two weeks the priest led prayers and hymn-singing which grew softer as one after another died. Maximilian was the last to die. To speed things up he was given an injection in his left arm. With a prayer on his lips he stretched out his arm to the executioner. Six years later the process for his canonisation began. This finally took place in 1982, when the Polish Pope John Paul II celebrated the Mass of Canonisation in Rome, so that he is accepted as a Saint in the Roman Catholic Church.

Ethnic cleansing

This is a comparatively new term now being used to describe the violent removal of groups of people from geographical areas, on the grounds of their different race, culture, or religion. The term is used, for example, of the Christian Serb persecution of Muslims in former Yugoslavia. Sixty years earlier Hitler aimed to remove Jews, Poles and Gypsies from Germany in the same crazed determination to create a superior race. It is a cause for shame that Christians take part in such evil thinking.

What the Scriptures say:

Whoever loses his life for me and for the Gospel will save it. Mark 8:35

Standing close to Jesus' cross [was] his mother . . . John 19:25

Summary

1894 Raymond Kolbe born in Poland

1906 School in Lwow

1910 Entered Franciscan seminary
Took the name Maximilian

1912 To Rome to study

1918 Ordained priest in Rome

1919 Returned to Poland
Worked as religious journalist

1927 Founded Niepokalanov

1930 Mission to Japan

1936 Recalled to Poland

1941 (February) Arrested by SS

1941 (August) Killed in Auschwitz

Quick questions

1. Describe the early life of Maximilian Kolbe.
2. Describe his death as a martyr.
3. In what way did Father Maximilian influence the whole of Poland?
4. What is 'ethnic cleansing'?
5. Do you think the media today could influence the way people understand religion?

POLAND
JAPAN
MAXIMILIAN
KOLBE
B•1894•D•1941•

OSCAR
ROMERO
B·1917·D·1980

ARCHBISHOP OSCAR ROMERO

Because of his faith in God, Romero denounced our country's sin with a fierceness which can only be likened to that of the prophets of old, or to that of Jesus himself.

Father Sobrino

The lives of saints always reflect the time and the place in which they lived. St Maximilian Kolbe is truly a saint of Poland in the 1930s. Oscar Romero was assassinated in 1980, in El Salvador. He was a saintly man of the post-Vatican II Church in Latin America, and is considered the father of the poor, their hero and martyr.

Oscar Romero was born in 1917 in El Salvador. He was from a simple background but educated enough to become a priest; he was ordained in Rome in 1942. He returned to El Salvador and as a parish priest he also wrote in the diocesan newspaper. He was known as a quiet, almost timid, very orthodox member of the Church and was not especially sympathetic to the **base communities** which were forming around him. He was appointed Bishop of Santiago de Maria in 1974 and three years later became the country's Catholic leader as Archbishop of El Salvador.

This beginning of a new ministry for Archbishop Romero coincided with the beginning of a persecution of the Church. He was 59 years old, an age when attitudes and mental patterns are already formed and set. The Church in El Salvador, like all big institutions, was powerful and immobile. The government and the military, until now hand in hand with the Church, were disturbed by ripples of changing Church attitudes reaching their country. In 1968 the bishops of Latin America had met in Medellin and decided the Church must make an '**Option for the Poor**'. Priests and nuns were introducing this new 'theology' into the slums and risking the anger of both government and conservative bishops. One of these priests, Jon Sobrino, describes in admiration how, within three weeks of his election as Archbishop, Oscar Romero changed. *'He became someone new. He acquired a new and different sense of what it meant to be a Christian. He understood his ministry as a bishop in a new and different way. He even adopted a new theology, much to the surprise and the alarm of those who preferred the old, the known, with which they felt secure.'*

On 12 March 1977, a Jesuit priest named Father Rutilio Grande was brutally murdered. His only 'crime' was to live in poverty alongside landless peasants. He believed that this is what Jesus would have done. His death shocked the Archbishop and challenged his views and his position. Against advice he ordered three days of mourning and a funeral mass in the cathedral. From that moment he became the fearless 'voice of the voiceless'. He saw in them the disfigured face of Christ and he re-thought his theology to understand that there could be no compromise with the world of politics. He saw his faith and loyalty to God and the Church as needing to be lived out within the politics of his country. As Archbishop he had an obligation to be one with his people – and the majority were oppressed and suffering.

For three years the Archbishop was a fearless leader. He wrote letters to governments and the military. He condemned the concentration of wealth in the hands of the few. He preached consistently about the rights of the poor, and he spoke out against the brutality of the USA-financed security forces. He was too much of a threat to the government and had to be silenced. He was gunned down as he preached at Mass on 24 March 1980. His people regard him as a martyr.

What Archbishop Romero said:

We must not seek the child Jesus in the pretty figures of our Christmas crib. We must seek him among the undernourished children who have gone to bed without eating, among the poor newsboys who will sleep covered with newspapers in doorways. Oscar Romero, 1979

On 24 March 1980 Oscar Romero celebrated Mass in memory of a local woman, Dona Sara, who had worked generously for others. The following words are from this sermon.

Those who surrender to the service of people through love of Christ will live like the grain of wheat that dies. It only apparently dies. The harvest comes because the grain of wheat dies. The earth allows itself to be sacrificed, broken; only in being broken does it produce the harvest . . .

I implore all of you, beloved brothers and sisters, to . . . have hope, joined with a spirit of surrender and sacrifice. We must do what we can. All of us can do something. Maybe this blessed woman that we are remembering today could not do things directly, but she inspired those who could by understanding their struggle, and above all, by praying.

Referring to the Eucharist, he continued:

May this body broken and this blood shed for human beings encourage us to give our body and blood up to suffering and pain, as Christ did – not for self, but to bring justice and peace to our people. Let us be united then, in faith and hope at this moment of prayer for dear Dona Sara and for ourselves . . . a shot rang out, the Archbishop died at the altar.

What others said about Archbishop Romero:

El Salvador has suffered a long and cruel agony. Yet one man [Archbishop Romero] stays in the memory as a symbol of Christian devotion and of unusual courage . . . To the end he was a faithful witness to the Gospel and he sealed that witness with his blood. Cardinal Basil Hume

If Archbishop Romero played a leading role in the Church and in society it was because of his profound faith in the God of Jesus. It was by being such a spiritual, such a religious man, such a follower of Jesus . . . that he was able to renew the life of the Church and guide the country along the road of liberation. Jon Sobrino SJ

Today he's not bishop.
Today he is Saint Romero.
And from his holy place
he walks with the worker.
From a base community in El Salvador

What the Scriptures say:

Go back and tell John what you have seen and heard: the blind can see, the lame can walk, those who suffer from dreaded skin diseases are made clean, the deaf can hear, the dead are raised to life, and the Good News is preached to the poor. Luke 7:22

Summary

1917 Oscar Romero born

1942 Ordained priest in Rome
Returned to El Salvador
Parish priest, wrote for diocesan newspaper

1974 Bishop of Santiago de Maria

1977 Archbishop of El Salvador
Fr Rutilio Grande SJ killed
Became champion of the poor

1980 Killed whilst celebrating Mass

Quick questions

1. Write a short account of the life of the Archbishop.
2. In what way did Romero change after 1977?
3. Some people believe he was too political for a bishop. What do you think?

Longer question

The poor people of El Salvador call Archbishop Romero a saint. In earlier centuries the Church recognised this as canonisation by popular acclaim. Should the Church today accept their judgement and canonise Archbishop Romero immediately? (Consider different views in your answer.)

SUMMARY ON TAKE UP YOUR CROSS

Followers of Jesus can expect to suffer. According to the evangelist Mark, a true disciple should anticipate martyrdom. Indeed, so many early Christians died for their beliefs that it was said the Church was 'founded on the blood of the martyrs'. The first of these was St Stephen.

For many Christians today faith in Jesus means going to church, saying prayers and trying to be good. This need not be very demanding. Jesus asked for something more costly. He said following him meant carrying a cross. People who take him seriously are often persecuted for the bold stand they take. Archbishop Oscar Romero is a recent martyr who defended the rights of the poor against an aggressive government. He believed that his Christian faith called him to defend the defenceless.

In the affluent western world there is a decline in Christianity. It could be argued that it is much more of a challenge to follow Jesus in a wealthy world. Wealth brings apathy (lack of interest or enthusiasm) towards religious values.

GLOSSARY

Acts of the Apostles The second volume of St Luke's written works in which he recorded the growth of the early Church

Base communities Active lay Church groups in the developing world. Catholics meet for prayer and Bible study and work for social justice in their local community

Ethnic cleansing A new term given to describe the violent removal of groups of people from geographical areas, on the grounds of race, culture or religion

Evangelist Someone who spreads the message of the Gospel. The name is especially given to the four writers of the Gospels, Mark, Matthew, Luke and John

Martyrs People who 'bear witness' to their beliefs by dying for the truth

Option for the Poor Catholic bishops' resolution made in Medellin in 1968, confirmed at Puebla in 1979 and later adopted by the whole Catholic Church

QUESTIONS

1. Read one of the Gospel accounts of Jesus' last days, up to his death.
   Write it up as a diary seen through Peter's eyes.
2. What is a martyr?
   Describe the life and death of a Christian martyr. Explain why he/she accepted martyrdom.
3. 'I can be a Christian without having to suffer. Surely suffering is bad.'
   Write two contrasting answers to this statement made by an English Christian girl.

ELIZABETH
FRY
B. 1780 . D. 1845 .

SECTION 9: FORGIVENESS

Forgive them, Father!
They don't know what they are doing.

Luke 23:34

Introduction

Forgiveness is central to the teaching of Jesus. Here we look at four different examples of how people have interpreted this call to forgiveness and reconciliation.

Forgiveness of sin is one of the key Christian doctrines. It lies at the very heart of the Gospel because Jesus made it central to his preaching. In fact, what he said about sin and God's forgiveness was astounding.

If we think about it there are various responses God could make to sin. He could

(a) explode in anger, outraged that his plans are upset
(b) be a little more controlled, weigh up the harm done and demand strict satisfaction
(c) be generous enough to ask nothing more than an acknowledgement of guilt and a promise to reform
(d) turn a blind eye and act as if nothing was wrong, offering total unconditional forgiveness.

Most Christians seem to believe God's response is (c). There are some Christians, however, who opt for (d). They point to Luke who described Jesus offering unconditional forgiveness. Luke reported that Jesus forgave his executioners without demanding a word of apology.

The parable of the Prodigal Son could be interpreted as a (c) or (d) answer. The prodigal son repents and is welcomed by his father (c). But the prodigal father is out on the road waiting for his wayward son (d) to shower him with love and forgiveness.

ELIZABETH FRY

Does capital punishment give security to people? By no means. It hardens hearts, and makes the loss of life appear light. It makes life insecure, inasmuch as property is given greater value than life.

There have always been people who have accepted the challenge of Jesus' teaching, and have gone out to help others, including those who have done wrong. Many reforms in the prison system were influenced by Christians. Elizabeth Fry is a shining example.

Elizabeth was born in Norwich in 1780, the daughter of a rich **Quaker** banker, John Gurney. In 1800 she married Joseph Fry, a London Quaker merchant. She was a serious and religious young woman, and in 1810 became a preacher for the Quakers (Society of Friends). A friend told Elizabeth about the women prisoners in Newgate prison. She visited the prison and it was a turning point in her life.

Elizabeth found 300 women crowded together in appalling conditions; many had their children with them. Elizabeth persuaded the prison authorities to let her visit the women and gradually she was able to obtain reforms. Schooling was provided for the children and the conditions in general were improved, because she made people realise that if prisoners are treated with respect they will behave better.

Elizabeth devoted the rest of her life to her prison work. Her influence even spread abroad. She founded hostels for the homeless and instigated other charitable organisations. This remarkable woman did all this as the mother of eleven children and the faithful wife of a husband who had gone bankrupt.

What the Scriptures say:

People who are well do not need a doctor, but only those who are sick. I have not come to call respectable people, but outcasts. Mark 2:17

Then Peter came to Jesus and asked, 'Lord, if my brother keeps on sinning against me, how many times do I have to forgive him? Seven times? 'No, not seven times', answered Jesus, 'but seventy times seven, because the Kingdom of heaven is like this.' Matthew 18:21-22

You have heard that it was said, 'An eye for an eye, and a tooth for a tooth'. But now I tell you: do not take revenge on someone who wrongs you. If anyone slaps you on the right cheek, let him slap your left cheek too. Matthew 5:38-39

What are prisons for?

Prison chaplains and other prison visitors sometimes question the policy of the Home Office on prison service. In what way does locking a person up (someone who is already quite likely to be disturbed and disadvantaged) solve the problem of crime? A number of answers are given:

- For protection: Violent criminals need to be removed from society for people's safety.
- For deterrence: Prison for some may well deter others from similar wrong actions. It may stop a person repeating the same crime.
- For retribution: Criminals should have to pay for the wrongs they have done. It will make the victims of crime feel better.
- For Reform: Criminals should be given the chance to change their ways and the help to do this.

What the Churches say

Church leaders and prison chaplains have criticised the way society deals with criminals. There is much evidence to suggest that revenge and retribution are among the reasons for sentencing and treating prisoners harshly, with inadequate provision for reformation and re-integration into society. Dr Runcie, a former Archbishop of Canterbury, said: *'Imprisonment in Britain is nasty, brutish and long.'* A Catholic prison chaplain criticised Catholics for showing very little concern for prisoners. He said: *'It looks as though we still find it hard to come to terms with the Gospel priority of serving the poor and the outcast, despite Our Lord's plain words on the subject: 'I was in prison and you did not visit me.'*

Summary

1780 Elizabeth Gurney born in Norwich

1800 Married Joseph Fry
moved to London

1810 Became a preacher

1813 First visit to Newgate prison
Worked for prison reform

1845 Died

Quick questions

1. Write about 100 words on Elizabeth Fry.
2. What do Christians believe about God's forgiveness?
3. What are prisons for?
   Do they work?

HELEN PREJEAN

It is in her moral and spiritual stature, and her actions in favour of Poncelet [the prisoner], that she is the face of love, the face of Christ, the incarnate Love of God.

Lloyd Baugh

In 1970 Britain abolished the death penalty. But this **capital punishment**, as it is known, can still be legally carried out in some countries and in some states of the USA. Debate has never stopped about the morality of taking 'a life for a life' as punishment for premeditated murder. Most Christians do not agree with this policy. They believe all life is sacred, and that only God can be final judge over life and death. Even the most depraved criminal should have the chance to repent and make a clean start. The problem is to weigh this up against the justice owed to the victim's family. They too have rights. If human life is so sacred it may be acceptable to sanction the ultimate penalty, death, to preserve the value of that sanctity.

One woman who has struggled seriously with these questions is Sister Helen Prejean. She is the American nun who has become internationally known through the film, *Dead Man Walking*, based on her book of the same name. Sister Helen describes the drama of her involvement as spiritual adviser to prisoners on death row. The film explores the moral issues of capital punishment and shows the triumph of Sister Helen's practical application of a Christian understanding of love and forgiveness.

Sister Helen grew up in Baton Rouge, Louisiana. Her father was an attorney and she enjoyed a comfortable middle-class life in a spacious home, with holidays abroad. Her parents lavished affection on their three children, Helen, Louie and Mary-Ann. Helen went to Catholic schools and eventually entered the religious order of St Joseph of Medaille. She wanted to seek (in her own words), *'a personal relationship with God, inner peace and heaven when this life is done'.*

In 1980 her community made a commitment to 'stand on the side of the poor'. Helen admits that this felt uncomfortable. She wanted a life of prayer, not the life of a social worker. On hearing a spirited talk about the injustice of poverty by a Notre Dame nun, Sister Helen was 'converted'. She chose to live and work with the most destitute in New Orleans. She describes her change of heart: *'Before I had asked God to right the wrongs and comfort the suffering. Now I know – I really know – that God entrusts those tasks to us.'*

Helen's work amongst prisoners and their families, and the victims and their families, demands enormous courage and compassion. She is not sentimental, neither does she 'preach' her message of compassion in an insensitive way. She has described how she tries to understand the feelings and experience of everyone involved in the situation. She is aware for example, that parents may feel that *'not to demand death, the harshest punishment possible, would be a betrayal of their daughter's (or son's) memory'.* Through her close involvement on death row, however, Sister Helen became convinced that justice must always be based on mercy. There must always be the possibility for healing, forgiveness and reconciliation, which is not offered in capital punishment. The death penalty smacks of vengeance and retribution.

What the Scriptures say:

Whichever one of you has committed no sin may throw the first stone at her. John 8:7

The film: 'Dead Man Walking'

The film, made in 1995, won awards for its brilliant presentation of the struggle between mercy and justice, forgiveness and revenge as portrayed in the true story of Matthew Poncelet. He was a convicted rapist and brutal murderer living on death row. Sister Helen Prejean was his spiritual adviser as he approached his execution.

Throughout the film Sister Helen questions her role on death row. She never assumes superiority or a cool conviction that she is 'right' to support the killer. She always offers compassion to the families of the murdered Hope Percy and Walter Delacroix. She says: *'Have I betrayed the victims? Do I have to take sides?'* The film shows both the unbearable suffering of the two families and the loneliness and abandonment of Matthew Poncelet. Sister Helen stands between the two sides, torn by her sorrow for them both.

The end of the film is remarkable in the way it introduces Christian symbolism. Just before his execution Matthew finally admits his guilt to Sister Helen; someone commented that *'the prison bars act like a confessional grill'*. She tells him that the truth has set him free and that he is a son of God. From this moment a bond of love seems to unite the two central characters. Matthew's last words to Sister Helen are, *'I love you'*. He goes to his execution dressed in white, the Easter colour of the newly baptised; and the death scene itself shows Matthew as if fixed to a cross (strapped down with his arms outstretched). He asks for forgiveness.

The film forces the viewer to consider the Gospel ethic towards crime and the sanctity of life. But it finishes with a paradox: Sister Helen is shown as the Christ-like figure of compassion and forgiveness, yet it is Matthew who dies, his arms stretched out as in crucifixion. No doubt the film has over-dramatised the actual stark event of this execution, but it leaves the viewer with an honest admiration for Sister Helen and countless others like her, who struggle to find the good, even in the most unlikely people and places.

Death penalty or not?

Christians and many others have strong arguments against capital punishment.

- Life is sacred.
- Execution is as barbaric as murder and other crimes.
- It is irrevocable and mistaken convictions have occurred.
- It is an act of revenge.
- It does not allow for reconciliation.
- It has not proved to deter others from murder.

The Quaker Community of Nebraska

Sister Helen Prejean represents all those Christians and other people who are willing to act on their conviction that justice must be tempered by mercy. In the State of Nebraska another prisoner is sitting on death row. He is Randolph Reeves, an Omaha Indian taken from a Reservation as a child by government authorities and offered for adoption. He was taken in by a Quaker family who gave him a secure home and good education. On leaving their home he drifted between jobs and began to drink. This pattern of behaviour is associated with the loss of cultural identity forced upon the Indian community. But his violent action remains a mystery.

In 1980, in a drunken rage, Randolph committed a double murder. His behaviour was totally out of character and he cannot explain what happened. He even knew the young women he murdered. Today a passionate campaign, led by the families of the murdered women and his parents, is pleading for the death penalty to be overturned. The whole Quaker community is united in their forgiveness and in their desire for healing. But the State Governor remains adamant that Randolph must die, as retribution. This is in stark contrast to the love shown by the murdered women's own families. Audrey was only two years old when her mother was murdered. Today she insists that everything she has heard about her mother has led her to believe that she would have wanted her killer to be forgiven. Audrey pleads for mercy as her mother's representative.

Long questions

1. Give the reasons why some people support the death penalty and why others oppose it.
2. Why do most Christians oppose capital punishment?
3. With whom would you stand in the debate over Randolph Reeves?

PONCELET
HELEN PREJEAN
REEVES, R
3 - 4 - 97
NSP # 33787

GORDON WILSON
B. 1927.
.D. 1998.

GORDON WILSON

His words, his attitude, his sheer human goodness and faith shone out like a beacon of hope in the darkness. **Dr Robert Eames**

No one will ever forget the standing ovation given by the immense congregation in the Roman Catholic Church at their commemorative service, when Gordon Wilson came in to kneel in prayer.

Bishop Hannon of Clogher

In November 1987 a shocking act of terrorism took place in Enniskillen, Northern Ireland. A bomb exploded at the town cenotaph during the Remembrance Day service, killing eleven victims and injuring many more. Gordon Wilson and his 20-year-old daughter, Marie, were at the cenotaph to pray for those killed in war. They were buried six feet under the rubble.

Father and daughter just managed to reach out and hold hands. In the dark and chaos of the explosion's aftermath, Marie shouted that she was all right, but then suddenly screamed in pain. She squeezed her father's hand and said, *'Daddy, I love you very much'.* These were her last words. She died later in hospital. Gordon Wilson, her heartbroken father, was badly injured. He amazed the BBC reporter, at his bedside, and the world that watched the television report, when he said that he bore no ill will towards the bombers. He did not pretend to understand God's purpose in the tragedy of losing his daughter, but accepted it as part of God's greater plan. He expressed his belief in an eternal life in which he would meet Marie again.

This unexpected attitude, this willingness to avoid bitterness and to forgive the unknown people who had caused him so much pain, made Gordon the 'Voice of Enniskillen'. It pushed him into the public eye, although he turned down lucrative offers from America to go on their celebrity circuit. Some people thought he was 'not for real' and waited for him to break. His health did break down for a while, but never his resolve to work for peace. His sense of forgiveness was undiminished ten years later when he died. What had given this man such grace and strength?

Gordon Wilson was the son of a devout Methodist and eldest of four children. His father was a draper and his mother a nurse. As a teenager Gordon was sent to the renowned Methodist boarding school, Wesley College in Dublin. He was a serious student and was recommended to study medicine. But on leaving school he chose to help in the family business in Enniskillen. In his book, *Marie – A Story from Enniskillen*, Gordon Wilson describes his shock on first discovering the harsh, biased views held by many in the North. At home his family always spoke well of both Catholics and Protestants.

Gordon married Joan in 1955. He took over the draper's business and she trained as a music teacher. They had a son and a daughter. A few years later, in 1967, Marie was born to complete a happy family, deeply influenced by Christian faith. Gordon quietly avoided the hatred in party politics. *'I was happy to try to be a friend to all and an enemy to none'*, he wrote later. The children were taught to be good to all people. It did not surprise her parents when Marie, a bright, music-loving, energetic girl, chose nursing as her career. She moved to Belfast for her training and was on a weekend visit to her parents when she was killed. Her heartbroken father described her as a daughter *'full of life, loyalty and love'.*

Forgiveness in the Middle East

Wherever there is war, terrorism or political tension in the world, there are courageous and saintly people who overcome hatred and distrust. Many remain private and hidden, ordinary people who manage forgiveness better than most. Occasionally, as in Enniskillen, an individual stands head and shoulders above the rest. In the Middle East one such outstanding individual is **Elias Chacour**. He is a Palestinian Christian who has a deep love for Jews and Palestinians alike.

His story is remarkable. Elias Chacour was born, the youngest of six children, in the village of Biram in Galilee. His parents were proud of their Christian heritage, which they could trace back to the first century; and they lived peacefully alongside their Jewish neighbours. Life was idyllic; the children were treasured and taught to love the 'Man of Galilee' who had walked amongst the olive groves and vineyards of their hills. Elias loved to sit on his mother's knee and hear her tell stories of Jesus. She could not read or write but she knew the Gospel by heart.

One day early in 1947, when Elias was 9 years old, his father announced that they were going to celebrate a feast. News had come that Hitler had died and many Jews would return to Palestine. *'We must be especially kind and make them feel at home,'* he said. *'This year we will celebrate the Resurrection early – for our Jewish brothers who were threatened with death, and who are alive.'* Many years later Elias described in a book, *Blood Brothers,* how the Zionist Jews came to the village, destroyed the houses, and took away the men including his father and brothers. The family was reunited later but never returned to Biram. Thousands of Palestinians were killed and nearly a million were forced into refugee camps.

In the midst of this suffering Elias learnt from his parents to forgive. His father would say: *'Children, if someone hurts you, you can curse him but this would be useless. Instead, you have to ask the Lord to bless the man who makes himself your enemy. The Lord will bless you with inner peace.'* The young boy decided from an early age that he should spend his life searching for an understanding between the Palestinian and Jewish people. He loved them both. He took to heart his mother's favourite words of Jesus, *'Blessed are the peacemakers'.* He went away to school and then, in 1954, to the Catholic **Melchite** Seminary in Nazareth. He completed his studies in Paris (Jerusalem was closed to Galilean Palestinians) but later he was the first Palestinian to earn a degree from the Hebrew University in Jerusalem.

After ordination Father Chacour was sent to a small village, Ibillin, in Galilee. He found a ruined church and no congregation. Today he is still the priest of Ibillin, but it is the centre of an extraordinary project. He has devoted his life to education and has built outside the village a college where thousands of young Christian Palestinians, Muslim Palestinians and Jewish youth from all over Galilee have been educated together. He speaks eleven languages but it is the ordinary people who love him. He has built them libraries and community centres across the Galilee region. Father Chacour gets little material help from traditional churches, who have not shown much enthusiasm for his acceptance of Muslim and Jewish children into the schools. American Evangelical Christians have been more generous. Elias Chacour is a brave voice for peace in the Middle East.

Quick questions

1. Write a short life of Elias Chacour.
2. Who was Gordon Wilson?
3. What do these two men have in common?

ELIAS
CHACOUR
B. 1938

PRETORIA
JOHANNESBURG
KLERKSDORP
BLOEMFONTEIN
DURBAN
ATLANTIC OCEAN
CAPE TOWN
GEORGE
PORT ELIZABETH
INDIAN OCEAN
DESMOND TUTU
B 1931

ARCHBISHOP DESMOND TUTU

Usually I get up at 4 am. It's quiet and peaceful at that time, which I need to collect myself. It's a time when I try to engage with God. I try to centre myself on God so that he influences the rest of the day.

In 1994 black South Africans went to the polls for the first time. The emotion of the occasion was captured on television when Archbishop Desmond Tutu cast his vote and danced for joy, singing, 'Yippee!' Alongside Nelson Mandela, the Archbishop has become a symbol of hope and justice for black people.

Desmond Tutu was born in Klerksdorp, South Africa, in 1931. His family was poor even though his father was headmaster of the Methodist primary school. One day as he walked beside his mother, a white priest took his hat off and greeted her warmly as he passed by. Desmond was amazed. White people did not talk to his people. The priest was Trevor Huddleston (see page 77); he was to become a life-long friend. Desmond went to stay at a hostel run by his Community of the Resurrection when he attended Western High School. He worked hard at this crowded school which had few of the facilities offered to white children. Desmond caught tuberculosis and spent twenty months in hospital. Father Huddleston was a frequent visitor.

These events and the political situation in South Africa made this young, intelligent student think deeply about his Christian faith. He decided to become a doctor but could not find the necessary fees. Instead he trained for teaching and qualified in 1954. He continued studying for a postal degree from the university and in 1955 he married Leah. (Today they have four children and several grandchildren.) They settled in Munsieville, Desmond teaching in the high school, next door to his father's primary school. Meanwhile the situation for the black population was becoming very difficult. In 1948 the National Party had come into power and introduced the **apartheid system**, under which black, white, Indian and coloured communities were all to live and work separately. The white population alone were permitted to vote, and had many privileges denied to the others.

The government made schooling so difficult for black children that Desmond left teaching to become a priest, hoping that in this way he could be a greater influence in his people's lives. He was ordained in 1967 after studying at King's College, London. Over the next few years he worked both in England and again as a teacher in Lesotho. In 1975 he went back to South Africa as Dean of Johannesburg. In 1976 he was made Bishop of Lesotho and was later secretary to the South African Council of Churches. During these years, Desmond Tutu was a strong opponent of apartheid, constantly in conflict with the authorities. He always preached a non-violent opposition to the injustices and with his smiling, buoyant character became an outstanding international figure for peace. He was awarded the Nobel Peace Prize in 1984 and the following year became Bishop of Johannesburg. In 1986 he became Archbishop of Cape Town, the most senior Anglican cleric in South Africa.

Desmond Tutu is best known today for his remarkable work as chairman of South Africa's **Truth and Reconciliation Commission**.

Archbishop Tutu and politics

Desmond Tutu's daughter, Naomi, recently revealed how hurt her father can be when his motives are questioned. He has been described as a politician playing at being a priest. That is a hard, unjust accusation. Throughout his life her father has preached forgiveness, peace and justice in the light of his love of the Gospel. His preaching is centred on the conviction that all people are made in God's image. There is no way he can stand back and see people treated without dignity. He once said: *'Our Christianity is not something we put on, like our Sunday best, only for Sundays. It is for every day. We are Christians from Monday to Monday.'*

When he was made Dean of Johannesburg, Desmond could have lived as an 'honorary white' in the official house, but the family chose to live in Soweto, the black township. His priestly role was to be with his people in their daily struggles, not to be a privileged man of authority. He says firmly: *'Religion is not a form of escapism. Our God does not permit us to dwell in a kind of spiritual ghetto, cut off from the real life out there.'* Desmond Tutu led the black people in demonstrations against the apartheid regime; he was always outspoken but refused to use violence. Once, when an angry crowd tried to stone a black policeman to death, he threw himself across the man's body and saved his life.

Archbishop Tutu believes that the Church has the duty to be the conscience of the community, especially where a horrendous political system is inconsistent with the Gospel of Christ. This means the Church has to be involved in politics. After the ending of apartheid and the election of Nelson Mandela as President, an extraordinary enquiry was set up into the human rights abuses that were part of South Africa's recent history. The **Truth and Reconciliation Commission** was chaired by the Archbishop. It required all the people who had committed crimes against human rights to apply for **amnesty**, and appear in public to explain and confess their actions. By doing this they would be forgiven and reconciled with those they had oppressed. The system was based on a deeply Christian interpretation of forgiveness. It was appropriate that Desmond Tutu led the proceedings.

The Commission's report has not solved the tensions and achieved the reconciliation hoped for, because few people share the vision of forgiveness that so shines from Archbishop Tutu. Throughout the hearings he wept at the scale of suffering described by witnesses. Yet he still advocates mutual forgiveness and reconciliation. One sober finding of the Commission was the general failure of the Churches and other religious faiths to challenge apartheid, with the exception of a few individuals like Tutu, Huddleston, the Catholic Archbishop Denis Hurley and a Dominican, Albert Nolan.

What the Scriptures say:

There is no longer any distinction between Gentiles and Jews . . . Christ is all, Christ is in all. Colossians 3:11

Love your enemies, do good to those who hate you, bless those who curse you, and pray for those who ill-treat you. If anyone hits you on one cheek, let him hit the other one too.
Luke 6:27-28

Summary

1931	Born in Klerksdorp
1946	Went to High School. Met Trevor Huddleston
1948	Beginning of apartheid
1954	Qualified as a teacher
1955	Married Leah
1965	In London at King's College
1967	Ordained priest
1975	Dean of Johannesburg
1976	Bishop of Lesotho
1984	Nobel Peace Prize
1986	Archbishop of Cape Town
1994	End of Apartheid
1995-8	Chaired the Truth and Reconciliation Commission

Quick questions

1. Describe the life of Archbishop Desmond Tutu.
2. What is apartheid?
3. What is the Truth and Reconciliation Commission?
4. How political should a bishop become?
5. Jesus said, 'Turn the other cheek.' Do you think this is a successful way of solving injustices?

SUMMARY ON FORGIVENESS

Forgiveness lies at the heart of the Christian Gospel. According to Luke, Jesus finally expressed what the Gospel is about when he forgave his executioners: *'Forgive them Father! They don't know what they are doing.'* Luke 23:24.

Perhaps the most shocking teaching of Jesus was his insistence that God forgives without any conditions – simply because he is good. Human beings find this a most difficult concept to grasp.

But Luke says otherwise. God is prodigal (lavish, wasteful) in his love. He forgives before the sinner even considers repentance. Few people achieve such generosity of spirit as this. Those who do, like Gordon Wilson or Archbishop Tutu, live in contentment and peace of mind in spite of suffering. Those who refuse to forgive can live in torment and self-imprisonment. Jesus wanted to set people free from such anguish.

GLOSSARY

Amnesty	General pardon offered to those guilty of political offences
Apartheid system	Former white South African policy of 'separate development' which discriminated against Blacks
Capital punishment	The death penalty. Abolished in Britain in 1970 but still carried out in some countries and in some states in the USA
Elias Chacour	A Galilean Melchite priest who works, through education, for the unity of Jews, Muslims and Christians
Melchite Church	Eastern rite Catholic Christian Church founded in the sixth century in Syria
Quakers	Members of the Society of Friends founded in the seventeenth century by George Fox. He saw Christianity best expressed in silence and simplicity
Truth and Reconciliation Commission	Enquiry set up into human rights abuses at the ending of Apartheid. It followed the election of Nelson Mandela and was chaired by Archbishop Tutu

QUESTIONS

1. Write a paragraph on each of the following people:
   (a) Elizabeth Fry
   (b) Helen Prejean
   (c) Gordon Wilson
2. Use stories and incidents in the Gospels to show Jesus' teaching on forgiveness.
   Why is it quite surprising and challenging?
3. Explain the workings of the *Truth and Reconciliation Commission*.
   Some people said it was quite unreal and unworkable. Would you agree? Analyse different points of view.

PETER DIED ABOUT 65 A.D.

SECTION 10: LEADERS

If one of you wants to be first, he must be the servant of all.

Mark 10:44

Introduction

It is hard to be a leader and remain humble, approachable and loving. Over the centuries some Christian leaders have been good examples of Jesus' call to lead through seeking to serve.

On a school-leaver's report a teacher may write, 'has good leadership potential'. What has that teacher recognised in the student? It is probably a combination of character and skills.

A good leader needs:

- to think clearly and have a vision of the way ahead
- to have courage of conviction and clarity of words in expressing it
- to be a good listener and a sympathetic, tactful negotiator
- to be tough enough to stand up to criticism and opposition
- to have organisational skills or the ability to delegate them
- to be decisive in decision making, whilst accepting the consequences
- to be realistic about own limitations
- to have great energy and enthusiasm
- to have a human touch and a sense of humour

St Peter, Pope John XXIII, St Paul and Martin Luther were all good leaders; they possessed some of these qualities – in different proportions.

Jesus himself did not set out these conditions for leadership. He asked for only one quality – humble service.

ST PETER

Feast: 29 June

Peter, you are a rock, and on this rock foundation I will build my Church, and not even death will ever be able to overcome it.

Matthew 16:18

Those who read the New Testament closely will see that the writers have gone out of their way to put Peter in the spotlight as the spokesman for the disciples and first witness of the resurrection. *'The Lord is risen indeed! He has appeared to Simon!'* Luke 24:34.

Simon is Peter. Jesus changed his name to Peter (Petros in Greek, Cephas in Aramaic) which means 'rock'. Jesus was predicting the fact that the impetuous, hot-headed disciple would, in fact, turn out to be the dependable, strong foundation of the early Church community. Simon Peter belonged to the fishing community of Bethsaida on the eastern shore of Lake Galilee. John describes how Andrew was the first fisherman to follow Jesus. He then fetched his brother, Simon, saying: *'We have found the Messiah.'* John continues: *'Jesus looked at him and said, "Your name is Simon, son of John, but you will be called Cephas".'* Simon was married and he later moved to Capernaum on the other side of the lake. Pilgrims visiting Capernaum can see an excavated building which is described as Peter's house.

The Gospel writers, especially Mark, do not hide the fact that Peter was not at all rock-like before Jesus was crucified. He seemed to speak first and think later. Jesus once told him, *'Get behind me Satan!'* Although he was one of the first to call Jesus the 'Messiah', he was also the disciple who kept misunderstanding what Jesus was saying. And it was Peter who enthusiastically promised to follow Jesus to the cross only to deny, three times, that he even knew him. When the going got tough, Peter got scared. The Gospels, however, make it clear that Peter and the fishermen brothers, James and John, were the closest friends of Jesus. Maybe Jesus had a rapport with fishermen because he had mended their boats for years.

After the resurrection a new Peter emerges. He is described in the *Acts of the Apostles* and in the *Letters of Paul* as the undisputed leader of the Twelve. He boldly leads them to preach the Good News; he admits Gentiles to baptism; he is imprisoned and, according to tradition, finally martyred in Rome.

Every page of the Gospels was written with the resurrection in mind, and none more so than the 'walking on the water' story. The disciples are in the boat and Jesus walks across the water towards them. Peter jumps overboard to meet him, but is frightened by the stormy waves and starts to sink. Jesus takes his hand and saves him. The disciples recognise him: *'Truly, you are the Son of God.'* Matthew's story (chapter 14:22-32) is clearly a preview of the resurrection experience when Peter is the first to grasp that, by holding on to Jesus, the 'impossible' can become 'possible'. The ordinary fisherman who had many faults became the bold, strong leader in spite of persecution. Peter is good news for ordinary Christians. He proves that saints are not perfect people!

Peter in Rome

A biblical scholar, H. J. Richards, has pointed out that *'the context in which the disciples first saw the risen Jesus was one of forgiveness. And this would come home above all to Peter . . . he not only deserted Jesus in his hour of need, but denied him three times.'* According to John, the first words they heard the risen Jesus say, were: *'Shalom, peace.'* Peter must have been overwhelmed at this experience of forgiveness; and it was decisive: it strengthened the renewed faith on which the Church was going to be built.

Forgiveness is clearly at the heart of Christianity. Matthew saw this. He wrote that Jesus gave Peter the charge to forgive, when he commissioned him as leader: *'I will give you the keys of the Kingdom of Heaven . . . what you forgive on earth will be forgiven in heaven'* (Matthew 16:19, author's own translation). Peter was a symbol of the Christian disciple – a weak and sinful person who repents and is forgiven. According to Matthew, the whole community was later given the same charge to forgive. *'And so I tell **all** of you . . . what you forgive on earth will be forgiven in heaven.'* Matthew 18:18.

Peter stayed for some years in Jerusalem where he led the young Church, helped by James. Others, especially the converted Paul, took the Good News abroad. But it was Peter who made the decision to baptise Gentiles, and this opened up the whole world to Christianity. He went on missionary journeys himself and settled in Rome. After his martyrdom in the reign of Nero, his tomb was remembered and honoured. The evidence of archaeology indicates that the basilica built by Constantine in the fourth century is almost certainly on the site of his tomb.

Quick questions

1. What do we learn from the Gospels about Peter's character?
2. Write a short biography of Peter.

POPE JOHN XXIII

Born poor, but of honourable and humble people, I am particularly happy to die poor, having distributed all that came into my hands over the years . . . which in fact has been rather limited.

When Pope John XXIII was dying, slowly, over many months in 1963, the whole world seemed to hold its breath in sadness. In the short five years he had been pope, this elderly man had captured the hearts of people both in and outside the Catholic Church.

Angelo Giuseppe Roncalli was one of thirteen children born to Giovanni-Battista and Marianna, small farmers on rented land in Sotte il Monte, south of Lake Como in northern Italy. Angelo was typical of the region, a warm, laughing, short, round, bustling figure, who, when he was pope, resembled the medieval pontiffs – with his determined chin, his fine nose and his large peasant ears. His round face was often creased and transformed by a kindly smile and a fatherly love for all he met.

He was born in 1881; a clever boy, who after school studied in Rome where he was ordained priest in 1904. Immediately the young Fr Roncalli was picked out for organisational work in the Church. He was made secretary to his bishop in Bergamo and he taught in the seminary. During the 1914-18 war he became a military chaplain to the Italian army. In 1921 Fr Roncalli was called to Rome by Pope Benedict XV to organise the societies which ran the missionary work of the Church. His gifts of tact and diplomacy together with his organisational ability, made him a good candidate for administering groups among which tensions could run high.

His diplomatic skills impressed the **Vatican** (the state headed by the pope) and Pope Pius XI. In 1923, aged 41, Roncalli began a brilliant period of his life as a skilled and much appreciated Church diplomat, first in Bulgaria, then in Greece and Turkey, and finally from 1944 as **apostolic nuncio** (ambassador for the Vatican) in Paris. This was a delicate and difficult appointment as some of the French bishops had backed the Vichy Government which was collaborating with Germany. Roncalli used his tact and humour to break through the tense atmosphere of De Gaulle's new regime.

In 1953 he was made a **cardinal** and moved to Venice as **patriarch**. It was presumed that, at 72 years old, this likeable man would at last be allowed to serve the ordinary people he loved, as a kindly bishop devoted to his diocese. But in October 1958, Pope Pius XII died, and after three days of **conclave**, Angelo Giuseppe Roncalli emerged as the new pope. Everyone presumed he was a 'caretaker' pope, rather like the overnight batsman, left in to keep the innings alive until a stronger player takes over in the morning. But Pope John XXIII amazed the world. He began by breaking traditions – leaving the Vatican to visit the prison and often doing away with centuries of stiff protocol. He had great energy, writing **encyclicals** and creating new dioceses. Three months after his election the Pope announced he was calling a **General Council**.

The Pope's two important encyclicals

In 1961 the Catholic Church celebrated the seventieth anniversary of an important encyclical on social issues, written by Pope Leo XIII. Pope John XXIII took the opportunity to reaffirm the call for social justice against the background of the twentieth century and post-war Europe. His encyclical was called **Mater et Magistra**. The international world welcomed this enlightened contribution by the Church on issues of socialisation, private property, state planning and the rights of the individual. He introduced a Church policy on distribution of wealth amongst all nations, calling on the rich to support the poor. This was to lead to the Puebla 'Option for the Poor' a few years later (see page 93).

In 1963, whilst the Vatican Council was in progress (see below), the Pope issued another important encyclical, **Pacem in Terris**. It caused a stir, especially as the Pope addressed 'all people of good will'. He wrote about the dignity of each individual, which implies equal rights for men and women, for all ethnic groups, for all races. He defended the rights of minorities and called for total disarmament. In a new spirit of co-operation Pope John XXIII commended the work of the United Nations.

Vatican Council II, 1962-1965

Pope John XXIII will always be remembered for his courage and insight in calling the Council. He made the decision on his own, saying he wanted to *'open the windows and let in the Holy Spirit.'* It was the twenty-first ecumenical (universal) gathering of bishops in the Catholic church. Its aim was: *'to inquire how we ought to renew ourselves so that we may be found increasingly faithful to the Gospel of Christ.'*

The Pope's idea was to re-examine every aspect of life in the Church, from liturgy to religious life, from Christian education to ecumenism, in order to bring the Church 'up to date' with the world. The Pope called it an **aggiornamento** (updating). Committees and secretariats were set up, and observers were invited from other Christian Churches. From the start confrontation was inevitable – between those bishops who wanted to move forward with new ideas and those who believed the Church could never change. Several times the Pope had to intervene, and it was always to point the way to renewal and change. He did not live to see the end of the Council. Its work was completed by his successor, Pope Paul VI.

Servus servorum Dei

This is the title given to popes, *'the servant of the servants of God'*. On his death everyone agreed that Angelo Giuseppe Roncalli had been the ideal servant of God. He was loved by everyone; he had visited the sick, the imprisoned, the poor, his priests – ordinary people. He asked Catholics to treat all Christians as brothers and sisters; he even reached out in friendship to the countries in the Communist bloc. His words and actions raised eyebrows and warmed hearts.

Summary

1881 Angelo Roncalli born in Italy

1904 Ordained priest in Rome
Bishop's secretary and teacher

1914 Military chaplain

1921 In Rome to organise mission institutions

1923 To Bulgaria as Church diplomat

1933 To Greece and Turkey

1944 Apostolic nuncio in Paris

1953 Cardinal Patriarch of Venice

1958 Elected Pope, John XXIII
Called for the Vatican Council

1961 Wrote *Mater et Magistra*

1962 Council began

1963 Wrote *Pacem in Terris*
Died

Quick questions

1. Describe the life of Angelo Giuseppe Roncalli.
2. What are the following:
   - the Vatican
   - an encyclical
   - a Cardinal
3. Write about the Vatican Council.
4. Why was this Pope loved so much?
5. Do you think the role of pope is important?

JOHN XXIII
B·1881· D·1963·

ζω δε ούκετι έγω, ζῃ δε έν έμοι Χριστος
The life I now live is not my life, but the life which Xt lives in me. Galatians 2 20
ὁ Θεος ὁ είπων· Ἐκ σκοτους φως λαμψει, ος ελαμψεν έν ταις καρδιαις ἡμων προς φωτισμον της γνωσεως της δοξης του Θεου έν προσωπῳ Χριστου
The same God who said, 'Let there be light shining out of darkness', has shone his light in our hearts, & allowed us to see his glory — the glory in the face of Xt
2 Corinthians 4 6
Ἐχομεν δε τον θεσαυρον τουτον εν ὀστρακινοις σκευεσιν
...But we hold this treasure in earthenware jars.
2 Corinthians 4 7
PAUL
D· ABOUT·67 A.D.

ST PAUL

Feast: 29 June

He went straight to the synagogues and began to preach that Jesus was the Son of God. All who heard him were amazed and asked, 'Isn't he the one who in Jerusalem was killing those who worship that man Jesus?' **Acts 9:20-21**

When Luke described the stoning of Stephen, he added the words: *'And Saul approved of his murder.'* Acts 8:1. This persecutor of Christians was to become Paul, the great missionary leader in the young Church. Who was he? Saul was born in Tarsus about the same time as Jesus. He was the son of devout Pharisee parents and grew up with such zeal for his Jewish faith that he tried to destroy the beginnings of Christianity: *'going from house to house, he dragged out the believers, both men and women, and threw them in jail'* (Acts 8:3).

Saul had studied in Jerusalem, but never met Jesus in the flesh. He 'met' him in a different way. One day when he was on a mission specifically intended to get rid of more Christians, he had an extraordinary experience on the Damascus road. He shocked his companions and later, the whole Christian community, by encountering the presence of the risen Jesus. The meeting turned his life upside down. He was baptised and spent the next three years meditating on this unexpected fulfilment of Judaism in the life of Jesus. Then Paul (his new name) burst into life in the Christian community. He was to set it on fire.

Over the next dozen years Paul undertook three long missionary journeys, covering about 8,000 miles. He set up Christian centres in Cyprus, Asia Minor, Macedonia and Greece. He had wanted to go on a mission to Rome, but was destined only to arrive there in chains. His fellow Jews were angry at his defection, regarding him as a traitor. He was charged with treason against Rome in AD 67 and beheaded outside the city, on the road to Ostia. His tomb lies in the basilica of St Paul's Outside the Walls, and has the simple inscription: 'Paul, Apostle and Martyr.'

We know a good deal about the complex character of this great man because he left so much written evidence. His letters, sent to his Christian communities, fill a third of the New Testament. He is described by one writer as *'a tornado of enthusiasm and energy'*; St Catherine of Siena called him *Quel Paoluccio*, 'That darling Paul'. Paul was sometimes harsh and unbending when his authority was questioned, and yet his letters are full of warm and tender messages to the ordinary people he met on his travels, housewives, dock workers or scholars. His letters are not easy reading because he often breaks into theological arguments. But he always offered down-to-earth practical advice to his distant parishioners.

Paul stands alongside Peter as the co-founder of the infant Church. Christianity could have remained a sect within Judaism, but it was Paul, the enthusiastic Jew, who saw most clearly from the moment of his conversion on the Damascus road, that Jesus lived on through his Spirit in the Church. He put his whole heart into taking that message out into the known world.

Paul and his letters

'Whenever I hear the letters of Paul read out in the liturgy, I am filled with joy. I thrill every time I hear his call ringing out. My heart beats faster every time I recognise his voice. He seems to come into our very midst, and to be speaking in this church.' St Chrysostom, fourth century

Many people, like this early saint, love the writings of Paul. Others find his words complex and therefore dull. Not everything he wrote appears relevant to this century. His writings were never planned; they arose out of the situations his '**churches**' found themselves in. He called the groups of believers that he had established and visited 'churches'. His letters were written 'off-the-cuff' and some seem to have been composed as he paced up and down, dictating at speed. Now and again he works a theological point out as he is writing. The results are passionate, if occasionally confusing.

A second-century document describes Paul as *'small of stature, balding, bow legs, large eyes, eyebrows meeting and nose slightly hooked. His appearance was full of grace: sometimes he looked more like an angel than a man'.* St John Chrysostom agrees that he was a small man, but describes him as *'five foot high, but with a reach beyond the stars'.*

Paul probably wrote his letters in the following order:

Writing from Corinth

AD 50 1 Thessalonians
AD 51 2 Thessalonians
AD 56 Galatians
AD 57 Romans

Writing from Ephesus

AD 56 1 Corinthians
AD 57 2 Corinthians
AD 57 Philippians

Writing from Rome

AD 62 Colossians
AD 62 Philemon
? AD 62 Ephesians
? AD 66 1 Timothy
? AD 66 2 Timothy
? AD 66 Titus

Love is patient, love is kind.
It does not envy, it does not boast,
it is not proud.
It is not rude, it is not self-seeking,
it is not easily angered,
it keeps no record of wrongs.
Love does not delight in evil,
but rejoices with the truth.
It always protects, always trusts,
always hopes, always perseveres.
Love never fails.

1 Corinthians 13:4-7

Paul and missionaries

'There are different ways of serving, but the same Lord is served. There are different abilities to perform service, but the same God gives ability to all for their particular service.'

1 Corinthians 12:5-6

Paul said that every Christian had a special part to play in the Church. He told the Ephesians that the Christian community was the **Body of Christ**. Christ was the head of the body, and each member was appointed to a special service: *'So when each part works as it should, the whole body grows and builds itself up through love'* (Ephesians 4:16).

Paul's special part in building up the Body of Christ was missionary work. As we have seen, he was largely responsible for Christianity spreading to the ends of the Roman Empire. He believed that the Holy Spirit was working in him and in the Church. Paul was the first great missionary **apostle** (the word means *sent out*) and the inspiration for all those who followed him. (See Trevor Huddleston, page 77; Mother Teresa, page 65; Sean Devereux, page 85; Sister Ita, page 93.)

Quick questions

1. Who was Saul? How did he change?
2. Describe the missionary work of St Paul.
3. What did Paul mean by the 'Body of Christ'?

MARTIN LUTHER

I cannot give credence either to the Pope or to councils alone. I am bound by Scripture; my conscience is the prisoner of the word of God. I can do no other.

Martin Luther was born in Eisleben, the son of a miner. After school in Magdeburg and Eisenach he studied at the University of Erfurt. He entered the Augustinian monastery there. In 1507, aged 24, he was ordained priest. He was a powerful preacher and a serious thinker, becoming the professor of philosophy and biblical studies at Wittenberg University.

As a devout monk Martin Luther became very anxious about the blatant corruption in the Catholic Church. In 1510 he left Germany to spend two years in Rome. He was horrified by his experience, especially at the Pope's efforts to gain money for the Church through 'selling' indulgences. Indulgences were promises of remission of punishment due to sin, following the individual's repentance. Abuses had crept in, and led to what seemed like 'buying and selling' places in heaven. It was a scandal and Luther had reason to be alarmed. On his return to Germany he began to protest publicly. He challenged the Dominican priest, Johann Tetzel, who was 'advertising' the indulgences.

In 1517, in a great public act, Martin Luther nailed his objections – his famous Ninety-five Theses – to the door of Wittenberg church. By this time he had many followers. He was summoned to Rome to answer for his actions, but he returned home to attack the papal system more strongly than ever. He preached passionately; he published works attacking many of the Catholic doctrines; and when Rome replied with forty-two theses against him, he burned the document in public. The Emperor Charles V supported the Pope, and in the fierce controversy that had developed, decided to act. In 1521 Charles called Luther to Worms in Germany where he was asked to retract his objections to Rome. Luther refused and so was banned in the Empire and put under 'house arrest'.

Martin Luther had originally only intended to call for reform. What now emerged was schism (a split) in the Church. Theologians took sides. The Dutch theologian Erasmus supported Luther at first, but finally left him as the former Augustinian monk became more extreme in his convictions. In 1525 Luther married a former nun, Katherine von Bora. He continued to be preoccupied with the underlying cause of corruption in the Catholic Church, which he now claimed was based on false doctrine. He taught that faith alone is the key to salvation, not good works. He rejected all but two of the seven sacraments: Baptism and Eucharist. Above all, he emphasised the importance of individual conscience and responsibility for a personal relationship with God.

The final split came in 1530 with the publication of the Augsburg Confession – the definitive statement of faith of the German **Reformation**. By the time Luther died in 1546, his followers were many. Today the Lutheran Church, with its 70 million members, is the largest of the Protestant Churches.

The Protestant Reformation

The Reformation theologians struggled to get the balance between God's sovereignty, and human freedom and responsibility. Catholics and Protestants held both beliefs firmly, but differed in emphasis. Luther's protests gave Protestantism its name. Luther was a man of enormous energy and had the power to set others on fire with his own convictions. He was a serious thinker and a troubled man; it is not easy to stand by personal beliefs against a massive institution like Rome.

John Calvin is the co-founder of the Protestant Reformation. He was a French Catholic, a student of law and theology. In 1533 he came across Luther's teaching and he joined the Reform movement. He wrote a defence of the new ideas in simple language. Rome replied by burning his works in Paris. Calvin went into exile in Geneva. He gave greater importance than Luther to Church organisation. Most Reformed Churches today (for example, the Dutch Reformed Church and the Scottish Presbyterian Church) are modelled on his ideas. Calvinism gave rise to an austere and sombre code of morality, which for a long time coloured Protestant Church life and social attitudes.

Summary

1483 Born in Eisleben, Germany

1501 At the University of Erfurt
Entered Augustinian monastery

1507 Ordained priest

1508 Lecturer in philosophy and scripture at Wittenberg

1510 Two years in Rome

1512 First protests against Rome

1517 Ninety-five theses (against indulgences) nailed on church door

1518 Summoned to Rome

1520 Published works attacking Roman doctrine.

1521 Luther banned in empire

1525 Married Katherine von Bora

1530 Augsburg Confession - German Reformation complete

1546 Died in Eisleben

Quick questions

1. Who was Martin Luther?
2. What did he protest about?
3. Who was Calvin?
4. Do you think the reformers were justified in protesting against Rome?
5. Do you think that the Church today needs a reformation?

MARTIN LUTHER
B• 1483 • D• 1546 •

SUMMARY ON LEADERS

Good leadership is always essential. Some say, for example, schools are only as good as the headteacher. Business succeeds when leaders have vision and insight. Lists of qualities thought to be needed for good leadership are drawn up by interviewing/selection bodies and by training groups.

Jesus did not have such detailed requirements. He simply asked his twelve apostles, the future leaders of the Church, to offer humble service. *'Whoever wants to be first must place himself last of all and be the servant of all.'* Mark 9:35.

Jesus led by example; he even washed his disciples' feet (to the horror of Peter). Later Peter became the spokesman for the apostles and with Paul guided the early Christians as the Church took shape.

Successors of the apostles have been good and bad leaders. Those who have served others (Pope John XXIII is a good example) rather than look for power, are the most respected and best remembered.

GLOSSARY

Aggiornamento Pope John XXIII's description of the Second Vatican Council. It means *updating*

Apostle A Greek word meaning *sent out*. Name given to the twelve friends of Jesus, sent out with the Good News

Apostolic Nuncio The Pope's diplomatic representative who is equivalent to an ambassador.

Body of Christ and **Church** St Paul used both terms to describe the Christian community

Cardinal Highest office in the Catholic Church next to the Pope. Cardinals are chosen from the bishops to advise the Pope

Conclave Vatican meeting of cardinals to elect a new pope

Encyclical Letter addressed by the Pope to his bishops for the benefit of the people

General Council Gathering of Catholic bishops to discuss doctrine and policy

Patriarch Title given to the national Church leader in the Eastern Orthodox Church. In the Catholic Church an ancient title given to Cardinal Archbishops of Venice

Pope Leader of the Catholic Church

Reformation The movement, in the sixteenth century, to *protest* against and *reform* the failures of the Catholic Church (hence Protestantism)

Vatican The state, situated in Rome, headed by the Pope

QUESTIONS

1. What qualities do you think make a good leader?
   Describe the character of Peter.
   Why did Jesus call him a rock?
2. Who was St Paul?
   How important was he in the early Church?
3. Jesus said his leaders should be good servants. What do you think that means in practice? Explore different opinions in your answer and use real examples of leaders where you can.

MARY, MOTHER OF JESUS

A woman spoke up from the crowd . . . 'How happy is the woman who bore you and nursed you'. But Jesus answered, 'Rather, how happy are those who hear the word of God and obey it!' Luke 11:27-28

Rejoice, in sharing God's own secret,
rejoice, for faith in silent mystery.
Rejoice, first of Christ's great wonders,
rejoice, fulfilling all his teachings.
Rejoice, maiden bride.
Sixth-century Akathistos hymn to Mary

Mary has always held a prominent position in Christian belief. Many disciples of Jesus have seen in her the most faithful and perfect example of a person living in the Kingdom of God. Her holiness and blessedness come from her unique position as the human mother of Jesus, Son of God. Orthodox Christians always portray Mary in their icons as a mother. She is never represented on her own, but always carries the child Jesus. The icon above is a typical Russian one of the eighteenth century. It was in the twelfth century when the humanity of Jesus was explored and understood. For the first time artists represented Mary as a tender mother of a helpless baby. Orthodox Christians never paint icons of Mary on her own. Without the Son of God she has no real meaning.

The Roman Catholic tradition has always understood this too, but over the centuries an exclusive concentration on Mary exaggerated her position. It contributed to a split in western Christendom in the sixteenth century. Protestant Christians remain ill at ease with an image of Mary appearing in visions – on her own – and seeming to take a too central place in Catholic prayer. Some Christians accuse Roman Catholics of virtually worshipping Mary. But this is not the case. It is Catholic teaching that only God can be adored and worshipped. Catholics love, respect and honour Mary as the Mother of Jesus, Son of God. Most Catholics recognise the excesses of the past but remain convinced that Mary holds a special place in the scheme of things. Art critics like the late Kenneth Clarke suggest that northern Protestants have very different attitudes to motherhood. It is less emotional and not talked about. The Catholic influence comes from the Mediterranean. An Italian mamma is like the Jewish mamma. She is never very far from her children and is a firm influence; she cannot be ignored! Catholics see Mary like this.

A recent, comprehensive study of the Anglican Church (*Celebrating the Anglican Way*, edited I. Bunting, published Hodder & Stoughton, 1996) outlines the faith and life of the Church in England and abroad. It makes no mention at all of Mary. This shows the very different place Mary, mother of Jesus, holds in different Christian traditions.

Mary in the Gospel

Information about Mary is very limited. Nothing is known of her birth or her death. The evangelists say little about her life. Traditions grew up about her but they are legendary. Most of the Gospel references to her are by St Luke, who saw her, with her Son, as the fulfilment of the whole history of the Old Testament. His descriptions are as much poetic and symbolic as they are historical. But this means they are deeply theological – they are an expression of faith in the Son of God whose mother gave him true humanity.

It is very clear that the evangelists saw Mary as the first disciple and the most perfect disciple. It is not surprising that we can look at all the qualities of discipleship explored in this book and see Mary there, leading the way.

When a woman in the crowd shouted out to Jesus that his mother was blessed for just being his mother, Jesus replied that she was indeed blessed – but because she heard the voice of God in her heart, and obeyed it. In this book we have looked at ten qualities that Jesus recommended as essential for the Kingdom of God. Through the ages Christian disciples have built their lives around the words and example of Jesus, sometimes concentrating on one quality more than the others. St Francis lived poverty; Julian of Norwich lived prayer; Gordon Wilson lived forgiveness and Mother Teresa compassion. Many Christians see Mary as the model (after Jesus himself) for all these virtues.

The only reliable source of information about Mary is the New Testament. References to her are scattered. She appears as a pious Jewish girl devoted to the Jewish Law. She naturally expressed herself in terms prompted by the Jewish Scriptures (Old Testament) and saw herself as a humble 'handmaid of the Lord', open to whatever God had in mind for her. She was prayerful, courageous and always at the side of her son – even when he was executed at Calvary. According to Luke, Mary was present with the apostles at Pentecost, at the birth of the infant Church. It is not surprising that from earliest times a theology of Mary developed based on scriptural images and symbols. She was given many titles – Mother of God, Virgin Mary, 'Most Blessed of Women' – to show that she holds a position that no other person can claim.

What the Scriptures say:

Mary said,
'My heart praises the Lord;
my soul is glad because of God my Saviour,
for he has remembered me, his lowly servant!'
Luke 1:46-48

His mother treasured all these things in her heart. Luke 2:51

Jesus' mother then told the servants, 'Do whatever he tells you'. John 2:5

Standing close to Jesus' cross were his mother, his mother's sister . . . Jesus saw his mother and the disciple he loved standing there; so he said to his mother, 'He is your son'. Then he said to the disciple, 'She is your mother'. John 19:25-27

What the Churches say:

We sing in honour of thy Son,
O Mother of God, and in praise of thee,
his living temple.
He holds all things in his hand,
yet he made his abode in thy womb.
He made thee holy.
Akathistos hymn to Mary, Orthodox tradition

O Mother, worthy of our praise
who brought forth the word,
the holiest of all saints,
accept the homage we present to thee.
Kontakion XIII, Orthodox tradition

MARY
THE MOTHER
OF JESUS

CONCLUSION

The great challenge for Christians is that Jesus seemed to turn values upside down. The luckiest people, he said, are the poor, the persecuted, the unimportant and the heartbroken. In typical Jewish style he described the ideal candidates for the Kingdom of God. Matthew recorded this teaching in the eight **Beatitudes**. These were eight ways of saying the same thing: this is what it is like to be a disciple of Jesus. This is what the Good News of the Gospel is all about.

The Beatitudes

Blessed are the poor in spirit:
for theirs is the kingdom of heaven.
Blessed are those who mourn,
for they will be comforted.
Blessed are the meek,
for they will inherit the earth.
Blessed are those who hunger and thirst
for righteousness,
for they will be filled.
Blessed are the merciful,
for they will be shown mercy.
Blessed are the pure in heart
for they will see God.
Blessed are the peacemakers,
for they will be called sons of God.
Blessed are those who are persecuted
because of righteousness,
for theirs is the kingdom of heaven.
Matthew 5:3-10, NIV

The following is an adaptation of a prayer by Brian Frost and Derek Wensley. It is a good summary of this book.

Those who live the Beatitudes
We thank you, Lord, for those who knew that
they were poor;
the Kingdom of Heaven is theirs:
John the Baptist, forerunner, prophet, yet much
more than a prophet;
Francis of Assisi, brother to every creature under
the sun;
Ignatius Loyola, prince of paupers, missionary
extraordinaire;
John Bunyan, tinker, poet, prisoner for the Lord's
sake.

We thank you, Lord, for those who mourned
while waiting for your Kingdom;
they have found consolation:
Jeremiah, lamenting, suffering prophet
of the exile;
Mary of Magdala, whose tears prepared
your corpse for a new life;
Dante Alighieri, whose ray of hope transcends
the flame of Hell;
William Blake, visionary, artist longing to possess
the infinite.

We thank you, Lord, for those of a gentle spirit;
the earth is their possession:
Peter Abelard and Eloise, lovers of life,
lovers of God;
Albert Schweitzer, of masterful mind
yet serving spirit;
Simone Weil, waiting on God by waiting on men;
Good Pope John XXIII, humble champion
of reform.

We thank you, Lord, for those who hungered
and thirsted
for what is right;
they are satisfied:
Patrick, binding to Christ a nation disunited;
Thomas More, man of conscience,
man for all seasons;
John Wesley, disturbing the peace of the
complacent;
William Booth, General of God's Army.

We thank you, Lord, for those who showed mercy:
may mercy always be shown to them:
David, psalmist, who blessed your enemies;
Stephen, martyr, who forgave his executors;
Florence Nightingale, whose light shone in
dark places.

We thank you, Lord, for those whose hearts were
pure;
they look on God:
George Fox, pulling down the pillars of the world;
John Newman, cardinal of great virtue;
William Temple, archbishop, workman for God.

We thank you, Lord, for peacemakers;
they are called children of God:
Abraham Lincoln, dedicated liberator of the
enslaved;
Mahatma Gandhi, undaunted apostle of
non-violence;
Dag Hammarskjold, untiring servant of the
nations;
Abbé Paul Couturier, inspired father of unity.

We thank you, Lord, for those who suffered
persecution
for the cause of right:
the Kingdom of Heaven is theirs:
Peter, Paul, apostles, saints, victorious martyrs;

Thomas of Canterbury, tradesman's son, chancellor, archbishop;
Joan of Arc, Maid of Orleans, inspiration of armies;
Dietrich Bonhoeffer, philosopher, protester, prisoner.

With all these witnesses to faith around us like a cloud,
we pledge ourselves, with God's help,
to throw off every encumbrance, every sin to which we cling,
and run with resolution the race we have started.
We will never lose sight of Jesus,
on whom our faith depends from start to finish;
may he lead us on to share the perfection of the saints.
Amen.

The photograph above shows Stephanie Pinnington (see page 85) in India with the children she went out to help. She represents those countless numbers of Christians, ordinary men, women and children who, day by day, quietly live the Gospel. They will probably not be written about in the *Lives of the Saints* or be canonised by the Church. They will be lovingly remembered by the poor, the underprivileged, the rejected and the suffering people they chose to help. It is this simple goodness to others that Jesus applauds with the promise:

Come, you that are blessed by my Father!
Come and possess the kingdom
which has been prepared for you
ever since the creation of the world.
Matthew 25:34

INDEX

Acts of the Apostles 41, 45, 120, 148
African National Congress 78, 88
Aggiornamento 150, 158
Agnostic 37, 40, 105, 117
Amnesty International 107, 108, 117
Anchoress 17, 26
Anglo-Irish Agreement 111, 117
Anti-Semitism 106, 117
Apartheid 77, 88, 143, 145
Apostles 11, 158
Apostolic Nuncio 149, 158
Association of Co-Workers 65, 72

Base Communities 94, 103, 129, 131
Beatitudes 163
Benedictines 14
Black Power Movement 81, 88
Bloom, Anthony 9, 13
Body of Christ 154, 158
Boff, Leonardo 105
Brazil 99

CAFOD 89, 103
Canticle of the Sun 31, 32
Capital Punishment 133, 135, 145
Cardinal 149, 158
Carmelites 19
Catherine of Siena 153
Christian Aid 90, 103
Christian Mission 27, 40
Christian Unity 111
Churches 153, 158
CIIR 89, 103
Civil Rights Movement 81, 88
Conclave 149, 158
Conscientious Objection 107
Confessing Church 106, 117
Contemplation 17, 26
Contemplative 26
Corrymeela 115
Cross, Take up your 119-131

Daughters of Charity 58, 72
Dead Man Walking 135
De La Salle Brothers 85, 86
Disciples 11
Divine Office 19
Dominicans 47, 55

Ecology 32
Ecumenism 11, 117
Empates 99, 103
Encyclicals 149, 158
Enniskillen 139
Equality 73-88
Ethnic cleansing 126, 131
Eucharist 129
Evangelical Christians 51, 55
Evangelical Movement 51
Evangelists 123, 131

Family Fast Day 90, 103
Forgiveness 133-145, 148
Friars Minor 31, 40
Fundacion Niños de los Andes 95, 103

General Council 149, 158
Gentiles 148
Gospel 11, 45, 123, 148

Healing 57-72
Heretics 47, 55
High Church of England 51, 55
Hospice Movement 68, 72
Hume, Basil 89, 130

Incarnation 37, 40

John Chrysostom 153
Jubilee 2000 90, 103
Justice 89-103
Just War Theory 108, 117

Kerygma 41, 55
Kingdom 12
Ku Klux Klan 81, 88

Lambarene 61, 72
Leaders 147-158
League of Nations 74, 88
Letters of Paul 153, 154
Liberation Theology 93, 103
Little Sisters of Jesus 37
Lord's Prayer 24, 26
Lundy, Damian 13
Lutheran 105

Martyrs 119, 120, 131
Maryknoll 93
Meditation 17, 26
Melchites 140, 145
Messiah 11
Methodist 27, 40
Miracles 72

Missionaries 154
Missionaries of Charity 65, 72
Molokai 62, 72
Moses 42

Nazareth 37, 40

Option for the Poor 33, 40, 93, 103, 129, 131

Pacifism 108
Palliative Care 68, 72
Pankhurst, Emily 82
Parables 45, 55
Patriarch 149, 158
Peace 105-117
Peace People 112, 117
Pilgrimage 24
Politics 77
Poor Child Jesus, Sisters of 33
Poor Ladies 31
Pope 149, 158
Poverty 27-40
Prayer 13-26
Prayer of the Church 19, 26
Prejudice 88
Prisons 134
Protestant 155

Quakers 73, 117, 133, 136

Reformation 155, 158
Religious Vocation 33, 40
Resurrection 124
Retreats 24
Rule of St Benedict 13

Salvation Army 27, 40
Servus Servorum Dei 150
Sisters, Active 34, 40
Slavery 74
Society of St Vincent de Paul 58, 72
Son of David 11
Son of God 11
Son of Man 11
South Africa 143
Street Children 74, 88
Summa Contra Gentiles 47, 55
Summa Theologica 47, 55
Synoptic 41, 55

Taizé 23
Teaching 41-55
Testament 31, 40
Theologians 47, 55
Truth and Reconciliation Commission 143, 145

UNICEF 85, 88
United Nations 74, 88
Universal Declaration of Human Rights 74, 88, 89, 103

Vatican II 149
Vincentians 58, 72
Vocal Prayer 17, 26
Voluntary Work Overseas 85

World Council of Churches 111, 117

ACKNOWLEDGEMENTS

The publishers wish to express their gratitude to the following for permission to include copyright material in this book:

Ateliers et Presses de Taizé, F-71250 Taizé-Communauté, France, for the song *Jesus, Remember Me*. Also for the texts by Brother Roger of Taizé, © Ateliers et Presses de Taizé.

Baker Book House Co., P.O. Box 6287, Grand Rapids, Michigan 49516-6287 for the extract from *Blood Brothers* by E. Chacour and D. Hazard, published by Chosen Books, a division of Baker Book House Co., 1984.

Burns & Oates Ltd., Wellwood, North Farm Road, Tunbridge Wells, Kent TN2 3QR, for the extract from *The Saints*, edited by John Coulson, 1958. Also for the extract from *The Popes*, edited by Eric John, 1964.

Catholic Institute for International Relations (CIIR), Unit 3, Canonbury Yard, 190A New North Road, Islington, London N1 7BJ, for the extracts from *Romero: Martyr for Liberation* by Jon Sobrino SJ, 1982.

Darton, Longman & Todd Ltd, 1 Spencer Court, 140-142 Wandsworth High Street, London SW18 4JJ, for the extracts from *School for Prayer* by Metropolitan Anthony of Sourozh, published and © 1970 and 1999 Darton, Longman & Todd Ltd; extract from *Courage to Pray* by Metropolitan Anthony of Sourozh and Georges Lefebvre, published and © 1973, 1980 and 1984 by Darton, Longman & Todd Ltd, and the extracts from *Good Friday People* by Sheila Cassidy, published and © 1991 Darton, Longman & Todd Ltd. Used by permission of the publisher.

Hodder & Stoughton Ltd, 338 Euston Road, London NW1 3BH, for the extract from *Celebrating the Anglican Way*, edited by Ian Bunting, 1996.

Bruce Kent for the extract from *Twentieth Century Martyrs: Franz Jaegerstatter*, CTS, 1997.

The Little Sisters of Jesus for the extract from their booklet *The Little Sisters of Jesus* (Walsingham).

Office of the Secretary to the President, Dublin 8, for the extract from *Reconciled Being: Love in Chaos* by Mary McAleese.

Dom Dunstan O'Keeffe for the extract from *Gregorian Moods* CD (Virgin Records, 1997).

Laurence Pollinger Ltd, 18 Maddox Street, Mayfair, London W1R 0EU, and the Estate of Martin Luther King for the extract from Martin Luther King speech *I have a dream*, published by Hodder & Stoughton Ltd.

H. J. Richards for the extract from *The First Easter. What Really Happened?*, published by Twenty Third Publications, USA.

SCM Press, 9-17 St Albans Place, London N1 0NX, for the extracts from *Letters and Papers from Prison, The Enlarged Edition*, by Dietrich Bonhoeffer, SCM Press, 1971.

Mrs Jill Thompson (on behalf of the Literary Executors of the Trevor Huddleston C.R. Estate) for the extract from *The True and Living God*, Collins Fontana Books, 1964.

Brother Benet Tvedten OSB for the extract from *A share in the Kingdom*, published by Liturgical Press, USA.

Ware Carmelites for the extract from their booklet *Hands opened to let go*, Ware Carmel, 1997.

Alan Webster for the extract from *Julian of Norwich*, published by Quidenham Monastery.

All Scripture verses are taken from *The Good News Bible*, published by The Bible Societies/HarperCollins Publishers Ltd, UK. © American Bible Society, 1966, 1971, 1976, 1992.

Every effort has been made to trace the owners of copyright material and we hope that no copyright has been infringed. Pardon is sought and apology made if the contrary be the case, and a correction will be made in any reprint of this book.